LEARNING CURVE

CHRIS EVANS

ANOTHER
LEAGUE
BOOKS

ABOUT THE AUTHOR

Chris Evans is a sports journalist from Warwickshire who has written for several top titles, including FourFourTwo, MailOnline and the Independent. With a strong interest in football, Chris has travelled the country, covering countless stories and matches from Wembley cup finals to reserve team fixtures.

Outside of football, Chris has built a reputation for digging out unusual sport stories and is an award-winning editor working on several contract publishing titles. Learning Curve is Chris's first foray into the world of book writing.

ANOTHER LEAGUE BOOKS
Burbage, Leicestershire
anotherleaguebooks@gmail.com

Another League Books is an
independent sports book publisher

Published by Another League Books in 2017
A CIP catalogue record for this book is
available from the British Library

ISBN 9 781527 210684

CHAPTERS

Acknowledgements   **6**

Foreword by Bob Wilson   **9**

1   A non-league dream   **15**
2   Wembley ambitions   **28**
3   RIP Danny   **42**
4   The second coming   **50**
5   Bradley's halfway house   **61**
6   Two games, six hours   **68**
7   Friends reunited   **80**
8   A right to dream   **93**
9   All roads lead to Rocester   **101**
10 D-day reckoning   **110**
11 Leading the way   **122**
12 In bed with Maradona   **129**
13 The campus champions   **136**
14 Spring of change   **148**
15 Olympic legacies   **157**
16 No more nerves   **166**
17 Gerrard watch   **177**
18 Track to the future   **189**

Roll of honour   **198**

Index   **212**

ACKNOWLEDGEMENTS

I was driving down the M1 when I first had the idea to write Learning Curve. I was just approaching junction 23 of Britain's second-longest motorway and my mind had registered the sign that displayed the turn off for Loughborough.

It was a town I'd only ever been to once previously, to cover a match between Loughborough University and Stratford Town when I was a young reporter, and I soon found myself recalling what a novelty it had been to watch a student team playing among squads full of semi-pro footballers in non-league. The more I thought about it, the more fascinated by the concept I became.

Sniffing out a potential story about Loughborough University's many nuances, I contacted the club and went along to the Scholars' next home match against Hereford. I went armed with plenty of questions to find out more about the club and, while the students lost heavily to the Bulls, the experience was enough to get me hooked. I'd seen and heard enough in those few short hours to know Loughborough's story was one that deserved to be told.

From that day, everybody at the football club has been incredibly welcoming, as they allowed me to pry and hang around (sometimes a little too long) to get the access I needed to put together the book. Loughborough's football co-ordinator Mat Stock was particularly instrumental in pointing me towards the right people and answering every single question I had about the club's approach.

As the months passed and the pages of Learning Curve started to take shape, I found everyone I interviewed – whether connected to the university or not – spoke to me with great enthusiasm. Without any of my interviewees, the book would never have happened.

A particular highlight of my time working on the project was when a hopeful request to Bob Wilson's Willow Foundation culminated with Bob agreeing to write my foreword – a gesture that meant a lot.

Behind the scenes, I received a lot of support from my better half Jade, who not only understood that I *really* had to visit a small village in Staffordshire on Boxing Day instead of continuing the festivities, but also put up with me rabbiting on about Loughborough at any given moment.

The support I received from the team who helped me put together Learning Curve has also been valuable – between Emma Bramwell's design work, Kate Feasey's expert eye to polish my words and Simon Kimber's cover photography, they've all brought something to the final product.

And finally, a big thank you to the readers, who are at the heart of any book. Hopefully you enjoy reading Learning Curve as much as I enjoyed writing it.

Chris Evans

FOREWORD BY BOB WILSON

When I go past the halls I was in during my second year at Loughborough, I still get the same feeling and chill that I did when I was there.

I attended Loughborough University, or Loughborough Colleges as it was called back then, between 1960 and 1963 and did a teacher training degree in physical education and history. It's a wonderful place and while it might sound over the top, I owe almost everything I've achieved in my life to my time at Loughborough.

I'm known as Bob Wilson the Arsenal goalie and for being on television for 28 years, but you can trace my whole life and career back to what Loughborough gave me as a teenager.

I must admit, I was scared when I left home for the first time to go to Loughborough. I was the youngest of six children and was quite a sheltered youngster – I didn't have a cocky confidence in myself. I'd always had a natural ability as a goalkeeper and a sportsman: I'd played for England schoolboys, competed in the English Schools athletics, I was captain of Derbyshire schools cricket team and was singles champion in tennis. But that all came out of natural talent rather than a belief that I was going to be as good or better than most other competitors.

What Loughborough gave me was a sudden realisation that I could compete at not just amateur level, but at the very top level of sport. You can't do that without a confidence, bordering on arrogance, and Loughborough somehow brought that out of me and helped me to instil a never-say-die attitude.

I almost never experienced any of that though. When I was a kid, Manchester United tried to sign me – at the time of the Busby Babes and four months before the Munich air disaster. England World Cup winner

Nobby Stiles and I were the two players United had picked out from the England schoolboys' team and my family had been invited over to Manchester for a charity shield match against Aston Villa. I'd been playing as a schoolboy attached to Manchester United for the past 18 months to two years, so I thought we were going over there to sign professional forms, which would have meant I'd never have gone to Loughborough. So it was a huge shock when, on the way home, my dad said that football wasn't a proper job and he'd said no to the offer. He told me that if I went on to get a proper job and then wanted to be a footballer, I might get his blessing. It broke my heart and I was in tears.

It became a choice between football and getting a 'proper job', as my dad called it. Our family had a bit of history in the police force and I was offered the chance of getting into the Metropolitan Police because of the sporting prowess there, but I chose Loughborough because I was this natural athlete who could run against All England athletes, and play tennis and cricket to a high level. I was also this lad who was quick, a good runner, had great physical prowess and this ability to dive at people's feet, which was the one part of my game that lifted me from the very good to the step above. Loughborough was the one place I could go that would let me see just how far it would take me.

That day I left Manchester United after my dad had said no to the contract, their legendary coach Bert Whalley said to me: 'Look son, never ever forget how good you can be.' I listened to him and thought he was bullshitting because I didn't think I was good enough, but it was Loughborough that made those words come true. It instilled in me that I could be a competitor at the highest level of my chosen sport, which became goalkeeping and football.

From the day you get to Loughborough, there's a huge challenge. It is regularly voted the best student experience in the UK and that comes back to the moment you walk in and you're thrown together with people. You just have this bond and friendship with people there, which will remain for the rest of your life.

Within my first season at Loughborough in 1960/61, I was part of the famous team that reached the quarter-finals of the FA Amateur Cup before our dramatic exit against Hitchin. That team nearly got to Wembley, and on the way we played Bishop Auckland and Corinthian Casuals, who were two huge names in the amateur game at the time – and we knocked them both out.

I can't tell you how massive it was. It was like Lincoln City going to Burnley and winning, it was on the same scale. It was national news at the time and we were being carried along on a wave that just got bigger and bigger. We knew from the amount of print there was in newspapers that we'd become nationally known. Everybody was so upset when Hitchin knocked us out and the run came to an end.

There is an amazing description of the day we knocked out Bishop Auckland. It was written by a famous journalist called Geoffrey Green in the Times. I repeated it in my autobiography: it's the most amazing description of amateur football at the time. It read:

'There is nothing like a change to blow away the cobwebs: there is nothing so bracing as something fresh and vigorous. A visit to Loughborough on Saturday, in fact, was a tonic: as much for the famous victory over those giants of the north, Bishop Auckland, that put the young Colleges team into the third round and last 16 of the FA Amateur Cup for the first time in their brief history in this competition, as for the spirit and setting in which it was achieved.

'Here in stark reality was David against Goliath. Here was an

outcome to satisfy the enemies of power, as the little man, for a change, came smiling through.

'Bishop Auckland have an unchallenged record of 18 Amateur Cup finals; they have won the trophy 10 times; they possess a well-appointed stadium that can hold 17,000, they claim a host of followers, most of whom, festooned and vociferous, made the 300-mile-round journey for this occasion, which no doubt gave them the right to let off some pithy northern comments, especially about the referee, as the tide for once turned against them. Perhaps it was the simple setting itself that made them ill at ease.

'There were ropes around the touchlines and not even a duckboard to safeguard boots from damp and mud. Across the 100 acres of playing fields other activities were in progress. Elsewhere, the Colleges' rugby football types were battling it out with the young medicos of Middlesex Hospital, the thwack of hockey sticks resounded in another direction, there were chaps in the indoor swimming pool, chaps playing badminton, chaps on the trampoline in the gymnasium. In fact, chaps everywhere indulging in their particular branch of physical education.

'Yet this day the real heart of the Colleges beat on the open field hiding coyly behind white and billowing awnings. A grassy bank to one side held most of the 2,000 spectators, strung out around the ropes. Among the expectant, noisy students in their coloured scarves were dotted proud locals, all united by a single hope.

'A wind whistled and the sun glinted between the flying clouds: on the horizon rose the outlines of a new student village of technology. This was the simple anvil on which was hammered out a victory that makes the Colleges a new force in the amateur *field. It was like some super-house match and Lord Kinnaird of old would have loved it, even if modern streamlined Bishop Auckland did not. Nor was there any doubt about the result!*

'The Loughborough team was R Wilson, J Detchon, J Henderson, T Casey, T Goodwin, R Ralfs, J Raybould, A Bradshaw, K Bowron, B Moore, A Brimacombe.'

The first year at Loughborough is right up there alongside my greatest, happiest memories and achievements. Believe you me, it's in my memory bank as clear as when Arsenal beat Anderlecht to win a European trophy, that crazy week when we won the double in 1971, and when I walked out at Hampden Park to get my first Scotland cap.

There were five or six boys – on top of those who made it – that could and should have had professional careers. Half of us were 18 and 19, and the others were out of the forces. That's what made that team, it was almost the perfect combination, plus the fact that we were led by Allen Wade, a man who was good then and went on to be technical director at the FA.

It was that camaraderie – and tuition – that made Loughborough what it was. As an 18-year-old just starting at Loughborough, I'd never have believed what has happened to me and the success I've had. Everything can be taken back to this jump in confidence and the belief that came from three years at Loughborough.

A NON-LEAGUE DREAM

It doesn't feel like non-league.

Driving along the narrow driveway leading to the cluster of buildings and football pitches that make up the FA's St. George's Park, a feeling of anticipation washes over me. Whether it's the setting itself or simply what it represents, there's a distinctly regal atmosphere.

There are the tall gates, embossed with the Three Lions crest, that announce visitors' arrival at England's National Football Centre, the winding road that leads you past seemingly endless green fields at a pedestrian pace and, strangely, a herd of cows crowded a few yards away. It's a combination of a country manor and a clandestine facility, set back from society to keep its secrets locked away from prying eyes. Perhaps the latter is exactly what St. George's is – at least in the FA's mind.

Trundling behind an ambulance snaking its way towards the collection of pitches, I try to drink it all in. Once I've seen the detail behind these high-security gates, no one can take it back.

I've never been to St. George's before and I didn't expect to make my maiden visit to watch a pre-season friendly involving two sides I have no affinity with. Yet somehow I find myself anxiously glancing at the clock on my car's dashboard to make sure I don't miss a minute of Loughborough University's clash with the Nike Academy.

As I watch the back of the ambulance lurch over another speed bump,

I peer towards the horizon for a hint of where the main St. George's complex will appear. I don't want to be late.

Today is the first match of a new season for Loughborough. It's a campaign I'm following to get under the skin of one of the country's most unusual football clubs. Not that many people recognise them as that.

The Scholars have been competing in non-league on and off since 1939, when a student team from Loughborough Colleges entered a wartime edition of the Leicestershire Senior League and lifted the title ahead of 10 other clubs. It made them trailblazers, as one of the first student teams in Britain to enter a senior FA league.

While Loughborough University – or Loughborough Colleges as they were known before the mid 60s – haven't entered a team into each of the 76 seasons since their first great adventure, the university proudly led the way for others to follow.

Regular competitors in the Midland Premier Division since returning to the semi-pro ranks in 2007, Loughborough University are fast becoming a non-league staple. Albeit a bit of a novelty to the teams they come up against. While most teams playing in the ninth tier of English football are made up of a ragtag bunch of grizzled part-timers who juggle their day jobs with life on the pitch, the Scholars squad have more spare time on their hands. They're all students and are part of what is as close to a professional football set-up as is possible at this level.

The starting XI's elixir of youth and extra time on the training pitch aren't the only things that make Loughborough stand out. After all, it's not every day that a non-league side is welcomed to St. George's Park to play a fixture of any sort, let alone a pre-season friendly.

The base for all 24 of England's national teams, and professional outfits paying to hold training camps there, St. George's' state-of-the-art site doesn't maintain its allure by throwing the gates open for just anybody. With 330 acres of space (most of which I feel like I'm driving through to reach my destination) packed with the facilities to give players and coaches the best grounding for success, it's an impressive sight.

Pulling up in the car park alongside the pitch, I look across to the main body of the centre. The building's glass exterior glistens in the sun and a stumpy signpost points towards the various football pitches, futsal hall and cutting-edge sports science facilities. It's a huge contrast to the corrugated-steel stands with leaky roofs and cramped bars that normally greet you at a non-league match of this status.

I head towards the swarm of purple tracksuits that adorn Pitch Four. Having battled two hours of heavy traffic to reach the touchline, I must have looked like the antithesis of the fresh-faced footballers who are readying themselves for kick-off.

"Sorry I'm late. It was the, er, traffic," I say, as I hold my hand out towards a tall twenty-something in Loughborough attire.

"No problem," he replies with a grin. "Although you have just missed my finest moment in football. We were doing a crossbar challenge from the halfway line and I did it first time."

This is Mat Stock, Loughborough University's football coordinator. Mat is the man charged with looking after me as I familiarise myself with the inner workings of the club's unique set-up. So, not only is he contending with my poor timekeeping, but he'll also be on hand to answer my constant stream of questions throughout the season.

A recent graduate, Mat works behind the scenes to keep the football operation running smoothly and has even found himself sitting on the bench as a backup goalkeeper in the past.

As we begin to chat about the team and the players I should be keeping an eye out for, a couple of familiar faces walk past in deep conversation. Norwich City Manager Alex Neil and his assistant Alan Irvine have a lot on their plates after the Canaries were relegated from the Premier League last season, and have chosen St. George's Park as the ideal place to take stock and mastermind how to make an instant return to the top flight.

"Unfortunately, they're not here to see us play," explains Mat. "Norwich are here for a training camp and the US women's football team are working here somewhere too."

The catalogue of high-profile company doesn't end there. Loughborough's opponents are also familiar with a taste of the high life.

If the name wasn't too much of a giveaway, the Nike Academy is a breeding ground for young starlets, funded by the multinational sports juggernaut. Made up of players aged under 20-years-old, the academy pick up lads who have been released from the sanctity of a top club and give them a route back into the professional game.

With a series of trials held globally each year to identify the world's best unsigned talent, the Nike Academy's squad list is brimming with potential. While a large proportion of the Loughborough players lining up tonight are students with little-to-no experience of being at a pro club, the Academy teamsheet boasts former representatives of Marseille, Lyon and Cardiff City.

The Academy's players aren't picked simply on past reputation though and count Ghanaian international Abdul Waris and Celtic midfielder Tom Rogic among their most successful graduates. In short, the Loughborough students have their work cut out tonight.

Mat tells me that preparation for the fixture has been a few days of intensive training and that this match is the next stage of a week-long slog to get the team ready for the start of the new season. Although the nature of university means that the first team can train several times a week during term time, it's not so easy during holidays. With players scattered around the UK and further afield for the long summer break, it's tricky to maintain much contact as the youngsters enjoy their time off. So fitness plans have been created for each individual and a few short bursts of training are being held, each punctuated by friendlies.

A trip to St. George's Park has clearly appealed, with 19 players warming up for the contest with their illustrious opposition.

"How did Loughborough get this match?" I quiz Mat, as the sides ready themselves for kick-off. "Why aren't you playing other non-league sides in the area like the rest of them?"

"Some of it is because of who we are and we have links with professional clubs or academies due to the work the university do," he answers. "Although the Nike Academy used to train at the uni before moving to St. George's Park, so we've got strong links with them."

As the referee prepares to blow his whistle to start the match, manager Karl Brennan gives some final guidance to his players. Then with a shrill blast, we're off.

Not surprisingly, all of the early running is made by the Nike outfit. Dressed in a slick white-and-grey kit, the Academy are well-drilled and zip a series of quick passes between their fluid forward line.

Korean Jae Heon Kim is the pick of the bunch and shimmies his way between midfield and attack with consummate ease. But despite his and delightfully named French winger Nassim L'Ghoul's best efforts, they can't pierce through a resolute Loughborough backline.

The long-haired L'Ghoul, or the ghost as the watching Loughborough supporters call him, slaloms in and out from the right wing, turning Scholars full back Toluwa Dada this way and that. But the young

Frenchman's desperation to start and end the move – OK, his refusal to pass unless there really is no alternative – helps his opponents out on several occasions.

Considering their lack of training before the match, Loughborough are well-organised, with centre backs Danny Brenan and Joe Jackson showing unwavering solidity to repel the ball as it keeps coming back at them. Brenan is tall and dominant, but still maintains a youthful look that gives him away as a student rather than just another of the huge centre halves that have called non-league football home for longer than they can remember.

Loughborough's best efforts to muster an attempt come on the counter-attack, as tireless forward Ben Ward-Cochrane ploughs a lone furrow up front; chasing long balls and flick ons in the hope that one will drop for him in front of the Nike goal.

Openings keep appearing at the other end though. And with only minutes left of the half, a lightning-quick interchange releases Kim in the area. The diminutive Korean pulls the trigger, but the ball slams against goalkeeper Conor O'Keefe's side netting.

More fast passing and L'Ghoul has space to fire away a shot. The lanky Brenan sticks out a limb and the ball flicks away towards O'Keefe's near post. Caught off balance, the keeper leaps to his left and pads the ball out with his palms. Salvation, for now.

The threat causes a stir on the sidelines, as Loughborough's bench give instructions to help their young hopefuls hold on. But the commands aren't coming from the manager, who stands silently with his arms folded. While Brennan watches on, there's another voice giving tactical advice to the youngsters out on the pitch. It's the chairman, Michael Skubala. And he's pacing around in the dugout.

OOOO

Michael Skubala isn't a typical chairman. In fact, he's not really a chairman at all. Dressed in a purple and black Loughborough University polo shirt and baggy branded trousers, Skubala's appearance instantly reveals his dirty secret: the job title is nothing more than a sham. After all, a university doesn't lend itself to a traditional football club model and is just a single strand in a web of organisation. Skubala may be registered as a chairman on the FA's official forms, but his role is very different.

"I guess my role is like a director of football in a normal football club," Skubala tells me when we first meet a couple of weeks after the Nike Academy match

"My job title with the university is performance manager, and I look after the football programme and its four teams. The university is like the owner of the football club, I'm like the director of football, and then Karl is the manager for the Saturday team.

"I've got to manage the budget on one side, then coach when I need to. With so many teams and players in the programme, it's important to get the right staff in and to make sure they understand what we're doing tactically.

"I'm listed as the chairman with the FA because it gives me the autonomy and responsibility for what's going on at the club. That's how I would describe the club in a non-league sense, apart from most chairmen don't really know how football works on the grass."

The same certainly can't be said of Skubala. At just 33 years old, he already boasts an impressive coaching CV that spans more than a decade.

It's a journey that started when, after being released by Nottingham Forest, the young midfielder turned to non-league for his kicks.

Stints at Hinckley United, Barwell and Rugby Town may have given him the game time that he craved at the City Ground, but Skubala knew by then that his real calling was on the touchline and he used the opportunities to hone his coaching abilities instead.

After taking his coaching badges alongside earning a sports science degree, Skubala soon found himself being called upon to coach his more senior teammates.

"I always knew I wanted to be a coach," Skubala continues. "I realised quite early on that I wasn't good enough as a player, so my attention changed. It sounds funny, but I probably started coaching when I was 18.

"By 22, I was helping the Barwell manager to coach the first team. He was more of a manager than a coach and I had badges, so I was asked to help out on the training pitch with the players, a lot of who were 29 or 30 and had played in the pro game.

"To do that was a real challenge and I had to earn the respect of the players a lot quicker than an older coach would have done. It was a great environment to develop in."

But it wasn't in non-league that Skubala got his first big break. Despite his own perceived lack of ability on the pitch, the academy reject's footwork opened his eyes to a new world when he was called up to play for Great Britain's university football and futsal teams. And after sampling the set-ups, it was coaching that pulled Skubala in again – with all roads leading to Loughborough.

"I've been here on and off for eight years now and came into this role two years ago," says Skubala. "I was doing some stuff with Loughborough University's football club before I moved to the FA to work on the national futsal programme. I still kept in with football by coaching the GB unis side. But it was futsal where I quickly progressed up the ladder.

"I came back to Loughborough to head up the futsal programme in 2012 and have helped develop 11 or 12 lads to become England players. I enjoyed bringing players on and the performance manager role here allows me to do something similar and transition players into the game higher up the ranks."

Talking in soft tones, Skubala is considered with his answers. It's a manner that's not dissimilar to his coaching style, as he carefully picks his way around my questions to explain how Loughborough's football structure works. All his responses are balanced and laced with information, and I start to feel like a promising fresher getting a personal induction to the club.

Loughborough's football programme isn't exclusively about the Midlands Premier Division side though. In some quarters, it isn't even viewed as the top priority.

Aside from the non-league team, there are three other squads that fly the university's flag: the firsts who turn out in the BUCS (British Universities and College Sport) Premier North Division and three other lesser-ability teams.

"The university has won the overall BUCS league 35 years in a row and we have no intention of losing that, so it's important for the football team to do our bit to help the other sports too," Skubala goes on to explain.

"We need to take BUCS seriously because the lads want to win things and we've got the university's record to maintain, but it does make it difficult when you've got a team in non-league as well.

"Most weeks you end up playing fixtures on a Tuesday night and Wednesday afternoon, which makes things difficult. It means that some Midland Premier League sides could be playing our seconds. In fact, one team even played our thirds last season.

"We split the first team pretty much in two to avoid that happening.

There are 25 players in the first-team performance squad that plays Saturday, Tuesday, Wednesday and we try to run it like a Premier League team would: imagine having Champions League and Premier League games."

It's probably the first time a team playing a mind-blowing eight promotions away from the glitz and glamour of the Premier League has ever seriously been compared to Europe's elite, but Skubala makes it all seem sensible.

Sure, Loughborough's students aren't playing anywhere near to the same standard as Sergio Aguero and the Premier League's other multi-millionaires but they're players who need their time managed all the same to make sure they don't burn out. And with the extra complication of studying for a degree too, no time can be wasted.

Just like a pro club, players' activity is closely monitored and Loughborough's raft of sports science facilities and willing volunteers keep a close eye on the workloads of the entire squad.

I once witnessed a Football League manager sending his reserve team out around the stadium on a match day to tally down all the statistics of the starting XI to collect the data he needed to perform an in-depth analysis of their performance. There's no such margin for error in Skubala's ranks, with his selection backed up by the university's extensive sports science and performance departments.

It's clear that Loughborough is more than just a good breeding ground for academic footballers who want to combine studying with senior football; it's a brilliant place to work in the back room too.

Out of the media glare of the higher leagues, Skubala's role gives him a unique opportunity to build up experience in a professional environment. But in the lower reaches of non-league.

"I'd like to be a proper director of football in the future," admits Skubala. "Then again, this is a great project and a great job to develop too.

"I've never had an interest to go into full-time football, but if I do the best job I can while I'm at Loughborough, then opportunities might open up that I can't refuse. I wouldn't compromise my life to have a tracksuit with a badge on it though – I've never done that and never will.

"I'm a trained teacher and did that for a few years at the start of my career. I'd much rather go back into that than chase something that wasn't really right for me."

○○○○

As the half-time whistle blows at St. George's Park, Skubala's teaching instincts are soon on show. The students have survived the Nike Academy's onslaught to make it to the break at 0-0, but there's plenty to learn.

While Brennan happily takes a back seat, Skubala's the man to deliver this team talk. With no changing room close to the pitch, the huddle is taking place on the pitch – midway in the half that the Scholars defended so valiantly in the first period. There's no hint of former Hull City Manager Phil Brown's famous on-pitch dressing-down though. As with a lot of things at Loughborough, this is about education.

Hunched over a white, magnetic tactics board, Skubala begins to dissect the first half. It's a detailed explanation including information on why certain things have gone right, where improvements can be made and how key players can get a little bit extra out of their performance. After each careful explanation, the performance manager looks up to find the players who are most impacted by what he's saying, and engages in a quick question-and-answer session.

For most football fans, the half-time team talk is shrouded in myth. Legends of rousing speeches that motivate players and tactical tweaks that tip a match are thoroughfare for this, the most sacred of times. The reality, it seems, is quite different.

As the lecture continues, Skubala finally poses a question that seemingly can't be answered by the group.

"Now, where's Ozzy?" he asks. "Ozzy?" But there's no response. As he surveys the players surrounding him, he finally spots his man.

"Ozzy! Ozzy!" calls Skubala, raising his voice in the direction of the near-empty dugout. "Ozzy, come over here. Do you understand what I've just been saying?"

Trotting over, tail between his legs, the athletic substitute joins the group, looking sheepish and deciding to accept the question as rhetorical.

"You don't, do you? That's because you've been messing around over there rather than listening with the rest of the team," Skubala scolds. "Now come on in and listen, this is important if you're going to come on."

The reprimand is short and sweet: there's more important things to dwell on and Skubala continues to chat through his thoughts. One-part coach, another-part teacher.

Despite the team talk, the second half doesn't start as planned. There's not a lot that tactical information can do to stop forward Joe Kouadio skipping to the byline and fizzing a low centre into the six-yard box for Danny Brenan to deflect into his own goal. 1-0.

To the Scholars' credit, the own goal doesn't herald a glut of second-half strikes. They're organised, resolute and close down Nike's skilful forwards at every opportunity. The visitors even threaten, with the pacey Dasaolu causing panic as he revs up to top speed, only for any half chances to be snuffed out.

"It's a promising start," says Mat, as the final whistle blows and the slender defeat confirmed.

"Some of these lads might not be in the first team this season depending on the new intake of players, so they've done well out there today."

This time, the players will be treated to the St. George's Park dressing room for the full-time team talk, as they collect up the kit and head towards the sanctity of the complex's central hub.

It won't be the first time they'll get to see what it's like to be in a football academy this pre-season, with matches against Peterborough United and Charlton Athletic's under-21 sides appearing on the schedule, alongside more expected fixtures to Midland neighbours Harborough Town and Redditch United. Whether the players realise it or not, it's a privileged upbringing for a student side that plays in non-league.

"It's just part of being Loughborough," Mat says, with another knowing smile. "We've got a lot of contacts and there's a network of alumni all the way through the Football League, so opportunities come up.

"Some under-21 teams such as Charlton, who we'll play in a few weeks, will come and use our facilities as part of their pre-season preparations, so we arrange a fixture as part of that. It's the Loughborough way."

Something tells me that this won't be the last time I'll hear that said throughout the season.

WEMBLEY AMBITIONS

"Last season, we lost six on the bounce to the start the season," explains Skubala. "We'd love to go and show people what we can do, but it's a challenge so early in the season."

It's hardly the rallying cry of Winston Churchill, but at least Skubala's being realistic. The Scholars are notoriously slow starters, with last season's travails a particularly painful experience for everyone connected to the club. With some of the team's best players graduating the previous summer and no reinforcements joining until the start of term, Loughborough's squad was seriously depleted for the beginning of the 2015/16 campaign. So a team patched together from a dwindling group of available players, who were mostly under 21, took to the field to face opponents who had been strengthening all summer. Not surprisingly, a string of poor results followed.

It's a memory that Skubala doesn't want to relive. But despite encouraging preparation and the new season's kick-off just hours away, there's a feeling that the performance manager still doesn't know what to expect come three o'clock.

"This year, we have 10 games before our term starts, so we're missing players who either can't get here from where they're living back at home or are away doing something else," Skubala says.

"The lads need to work, earn money and spend time with their family, who they haven't seen all year. Others are away travelling or on placements through the summer.

"We don't know how close we are to our best team and probably won't until at least September. We have got a few players away at the moment and will add as many as eight players to the performance squad at the start of term, so some of the starters today could bounce into the twos come October."

Skubala is at Loughborough University's eponymous stadium early, pumping up futsal balls from the boot of his car and putting the final touches to the preparation for today's curtain-raiser.

Dressed in the same baggy Loughborough tracksuit bottoms and polo shirt he wore on that unseasonably chilly July evening at St. George's Park, Skubala sips from a tall glass of cola as we chat away.

There's always an element of uncertainty when any new football season kicks off, but it's normally overwhelmed by a sense of excitement at what might happen in the coming months. Starting a campaign with an almost traditional disadvantage to the rest of the league naturally beckons some trepidation though.

While they won't be able to strengthen their ranks for another month or so, the Scholars also have some notable faces missing from the pool of students who are still available.

Goalkeeper Danny Wright, who would normally be challenging for the number-one shirt, is travelling in New Zealand. Midfielder Jack Poxon is on a summer placement as an investment banker in London – "he'll probably land a £50,000 job at the end of it, so we can't compromise that," remarks Skubala – and others can't afford to dip into their precious student loans to make the special trip across the UK back to uni for a single match.

As if the absentees on the pitch weren't bad enough, the Loughborough teamsheet will be missing another familiar name for today's match. If Skubala's attire wasn't a giveaway, he's set for another stint in the dugout, as regular Saturday manager Karl Brennan is currently thousands of miles away holidaying in the US.

Skubala seems laid-back about it all. A case of wait and see, rather than the usual burden that every result will mean life or death. Despite the lack of pressure, there's high stakes on today's match.

It might only be 6 August, but the clash against Shirebrook Town already has a lot riding on it. The FA Cup is set to begin at its earliest ever date, which means Loughborough's Wembley dream could be over before they've even kicked a ball in the league.

The competition hasn't been a happy hunting ground for Loughborough since they returned to non-league in 2007. From nine previous attempts, they have only made it to the first qualifying round of the FA Cup twice before, which is still four victories away from the first round proper when the first of the Football League sides enter.

With two preliminary matches in this year's competition before they reach the qualifying rounds, it could be a tall order for the students to even emulate their best performance.

"The FA Cup gets earlier and earlier, and that doesn't help us," reasons Skubala. "If it was later, we'd probably stand a better chance of having a bit of a run – but we're usually out by the time we're at our strongest.

"After our bad start last season, we were at the bottom of the league. But then when we came to November and December, we were flying and winning most of our matches."

The summer sun isn't greeted with much mirth around these parts then. Never before have I discovered such a lack of anticipation before the season begins in earnest. While everything is geared towards success on the pitch, a combination of the Scholars' early season struggles and their wretched FA Cup record means that a defeat wouldn't be wholly unexpected.

Perhaps there is hope. Opponents Shirebrook are from a division lower and aren't flush with experience themselves. And as the chattering students begin to arrive in their tracksuits, there's no reason to doubt that the class of 2016/17 can't buck the trend.

Maybe this could be Loughborough's year after all.

OOOO

If by some incredible feat Loughborough's students are able to launch an unexpected tilt for the FA Cup, it wouldn't be the first time that the university has flirted with appearing at Wembley.

Back in 1961, the Scholars entered a team into the FA Amateur Cup and earned national notoriety for their performances. To the backdrop of some controversy, as some clubs believed that a higher education team should not be allowed into the competition, they embarked on an incredible winning run that had many locals dreaming of the famous twin towers.

It was the first time that Loughborough Colleges had ever entered the competition, despite playing in the Leicestershire Senior League for more than 20 years. But a talented team that included a number of players who would go on to play professionally, such as Bob Wilson, Dario Gradi and Alan Bradshaw, made a big impression.

By half-time in their first match in the FA Amateur Cup, Loughborough were 5-1 up against Moor Green. A comfortable passage to the next round might have been on the cards, until the Moors pegged them back to 5-5 within 10 minutes of the restart. That shocked the students back into life and they bagged five more goals without reply to seal a quite remarkable 10-5 victory.

The match that captured the most attention was their second-round contest against Bishop Auckland, who were regarded as the best amateur team in the country at the time. That didn't deter Loughborough though, as they ran out 3-1 winners, earning themselves a special mention from esteemed commentator Kenneth Wolstenholme (he of the famous 'they think it's all over' clip as England clinched the 1966 World Cup) on the BBC that night and plenty of column inches in the national newspapers the next day.

Next up were another famous amateur side, Corinthian Casuals, who were also put to the sword in a 2-1 victory. So by the time the quarter-finals had come round, Loughborough were dark horses to lift the trophy – and with only two more wins needed to reach the Wembley final, the students were beginning to dream.

Sadly, that's where the run ended. When future Arsenal keeper Wilson was carried off with broken ribs in the opening stages of the last-eight tie with Hitchin Town, the Scholars were left to play on with 10 men and an outfielder in-between the sticks, as substitutions weren't allowed. Predictably, it didn't end well and they were left on the wrong end of a 5-1 scoreline.

The following year, they came up against Bishop Auckland again, this time in round three, but the northerners exacted their revenge by winning 2-0. The club only made it as far on two further occasions, with the class of 61 standing out as the closest any Loughborough team ever got to tasting cup glory.

While Loughborough's record might not suggest it, student success in the FA Cup isn't completely unheard of. Not if you're prepared to trawl the annals of football history anyway.

Back in a time of long moustaches and even longer shorts, Oxford University won the 1874 FA Cup with a 2-0 victory over Royal Engineers at the Kennington Oval. That's right, a team of university students lifted the famous trophy. Dressed in blue-and-white-halved shirts, Oxford's student football team were considered to be slight underdogs to get their hands on the cup, despite having reached the previous year's final, when they lost against Wanderers.

The amateur footballers who took to the field to do battle for the third FA Cup Final were scarcely recognisable compared to the preened professionals of modern day. Made up of an assortment of players with varied backgrounds, including a reverend, a future music producer and the nephew of a Conservative MP, Oxford's team contained a true hotchpotch of backgrounds.

The students were considered to be one of the country's best sides at the time, but were coming up against a Royal Engineers side who had plundered 16 goals and only conceded once en route to the final. The Engineers, as the name suggests, were made up of members of the British Army's Corps of Royal Engineers, so the final was to see two of the UK's greatest institutions go head-to-head for glory.

The university's chances of winning were boosted weeks before kick-off with the news that one of their opponent's star players, Lieutenant Alfred Goodwyn, had been called up for service in India and would miss the final. Goodwyn would never see any of his teammates again, after dying on the day of the final following an incident involving his horse.

While the two sides were blissfully unaware of Goodwyn's tragic demise on another continent, the students made a quick-fire start to the match – and were 2-0 up within the first 20 minutes, as Charles Mackarness and Frederick Patton struck.

The early lead would prove decisive, partly thanks to the heroics of 23-year-old goalkeeper Charles Nepean. Nepean, who was better known for his talents with a cricket ball, made a string of saves to ensure that the students would become the only higher-education team to win the famous trophy.

The result could have been greater, as the Blue reportedly netted a third goal before the final whistle. Although the ball appeared to have crossed the goalline, the students didn't claim for the goal to be given and in line with the law at the time, that meant it wasn't added to their tally. While the history books remain hazy about why the quirk occurred, it didn't cost Oxford as they went on to celebrate at full-time.

It wasn't to be the only glory the university would enjoy in the coming years, although they were never able to get their hands on the FA Cup again. They reached two further finals – losing 2-1 to Wanderers again in 1877 and 1-0 to Clapham Rovers in 1880 – and provided the springboard for several England and Wales internationals to get their caps. The 1880 final proved to be the last time that Oxford University would enter the FA Cup and so ended their love affair with the competition. So it seemed for student teams too, until 2002 that is.

A mere 128 years after Oxford triumphed under the Oval's famous gasholder, Team Bath became the first university side to reach the FA Cup's first round proper. Managed by the charismatic Paul Tisdale, who has gone on to serve for over a decade at Exeter City, University of Bath's football team earned national attention for their run and did the student name proud by pushing Football Leaguers Mansfield Town all the way in a 4-2 defeat. It was the culmination of an incredible run, which saw Bath beat five sides on the way to reaching the first round.

That wasn't the end of Team Bath's exploits though. They reached the Conference South, English football's sixth tier, seven years later, before their success story came to an abrupt end.

Using a different model to Loughborough, which included offering paid sports scholarships to attract players, the Crescents were told that they wouldn't be eligible for further promotions or entry into the FA Cup due to the club not being a limited company. As a result, Team Bath, who had previously been open about their ambitions of reaching the Football League, resigned their place in the Conference South at the end of the 2008-09 season and returned to the student leagues – closing the door on another chapter of university football.

OOOO

Dreams of matching the success of either Oxford University or Team Bath might be premature for Loughborough's youngsters, but as they exit the smartly decorated dressing room ready to face Shirebrook, they're taking the first steps on what could be a career-defining cup run.

The visitors, dressed in an all-green kit with white trim, march out in a line alongside their opponents. Led by captain Liam Osborne, who at a sprightly 28-years-old is the most senior player on the pitch, Shirebrook are cheered on by a rowdy bunch of fans in the main stand. The knot of away supporters make up a decent proportion of the 130-strong crowd that are spread across the elevated seats that overlook the pristine pitch. They have made the trip from neighbouring Derbyshire to see if their charges can pull off a relative giant-killing by knocking Loughborough out.

Although the history books might suggest the two teams are competing on a level playing field, the surroundings certainly don't. The uni's ground is based on the edge of the busy campus and isn't the archetypal location for a Midland Football League club to call home. Loughborough University Stadium was opened four years ago, following a £4-million investment, and has maintained its box-fresh look.

The all-seater main stand is the focal point, towering several feet up above the clean, metal terraces that run alongside the pitch. Tagged on to the stand is a set of fully furnished conference facilities, doused in Loughborough purple. To the left is a large, pine-coloured building, fitted with wide glass windows that offer a glimpse into the university's state-of-the-art gym. Ahead, more new builds clutter the horizon, while a large pile of sand – akin to an oversized anthill – signals that yet more facilities are set to spring from the ground in the near future. The perfectly mown pitch is in great shape too, while a tall electronic scoreboard completes the picture. If somebody told me this was the heart of a training centre built by a nouveau-riche Premier League club for their youth teams, I'd believe them. Beating Loughborough has all the hallmarks of a big scalp for today's visitors.

"It's like the Wembley of non-league," jokes a Shirebrook fan as he steps out of the adjoining bar to find a seat for kick-off. It's hard to disagree.

For all the realism that shrouded the match before kick-off, the students nearly get off to the dream start.

Midfielder Josh Hill, who graduated last year but is still turning out for the side before he dons his cap and gown, bursts into the area and is tripped by a Shirebrook defender. The referee points to the spot. Maybe the pre-match pessimism was misplaced. Debutant Luke Trotman is on spot-kick duty. The 18-year-old former Luton Town trainee looks resplendent in his bright-green boots and places the ball on the spot. Trotman has all the poise of a confident penalty taker, but is perhaps too laid-back as he blazes his kick well over the bar – triggering some stifled laughter among the supporters in the main stand.

It's not about to get any better for Trotman either. The full back may have made several appearances for Luton's academy side in recent years, but the difference to senior football is already obvious. A direct ball forward picks out Shirebrook forward Mitch Mullins, who is being played onside by Trotman and bundles past the teenager to unleash a powerful effort high into the net. The students are 1-0 down.

The hoodoo that Skubala spoke about before kick-off appears to be self-fulfilling as the visitors strike again within minutes. An over-hit cross from skipper Osborne looks to be drifting harmlessly away from goal, but keeper Conor O'Keefe somehow misjudges the flight of the ball and lets it drop into the net. There are a few grumbles in the stand as Shirebrook's supporters celebrate. Here we go again.

Skubala is out on the edge of his dugout, attempting to rally his ailing troops and his enthusiasm begins to have the desired effect. First, Hill forces opposition goalkeeper Jake Bedford into a save, then Trotman bends a mazy run into the box before seeing Bedford tip his strike wide. There are encouraging signs but, as the half-time whistle blows, Loughborough are trailing by two goals and facing another early FA Cup exit.

"I didn't expect us to be world-beaters today. It's always a slow start until they've got a full squad of players available," comments Loughborough local Dave Kearins during the interval.

Dave has been splitting his time between coming to the Loughborough University Stadium and watching the town's other club, Loughborough Dynamo, for the past few years and has already grown accustomed to the students' shortfalls, it seems.

"It's a good chance for some of the university's younger players to have a go now," Dave continues. "There are six or seven of the players out there who I recognise from last season, but they don't seem terribly well-organised at the moment and a couple of them are playing in different positions. There's the nucleus of a side here, but it's early days and they need time to gel."

The possibility of seeing a collection of young players cobbled together from the university's seconds and new starters doesn't deter Dave from coming along to watch though. It's the prospect of seeing the green shoots of August blossom into a competitive team that attracts people like him through the turnstiles.

"It's good to see the players develop over the months. As a student team, the youngsters are given a chance to play, so you can see them improve over time," he adds. "I just hope Loughborough's superior fitness will come through in the second half and we can get back in this."

As play begins again for the second half, Dave's wish might come true. Skipper Danny Brenan, one of the handful of players from the previous campaign, rises highest from an early corner and directs a header against the foot of the post. Despite his best efforts, Tom Barnes can't turn in the rebound.

The hosts are in the ascendency and speedy winger Jeremiah Dasaolu starts to get some joy down the right flank. The brother of Team GB sprinter James, Dasaolu possesses frightening pace, wriggling into some space in the box and comes horribly close to directing a close-range effort beyond Bedford. But a curse wouldn't be a curse if there wasn't a sting in the tail. Just as it looks inevitable that the Scholars will notch, they fall even further behind. Brenan stretches for a ball in his own area and trips

Mullins. It's a penalty for Shirebrook and Osborne nets his second goal of the game.

With 15 minutes remaining, Hill finally gets a goal back. The 24-year-old, who is Loughborough's oldest player today, is allowed too much time on the edge of the Shirebrook area and steers in a low drive.

It looks to be nothing more than a consolation until Drew Bridge sparks an unthinkable comeback. As the stadium clock ticks to 86 minutes, the forward gets free to head home a second. And then, moments later, the same player is given the chance to level from the spot after Brenan is shoved over. Bridge converts to complete the comeback: it's 3-3.

The equaliser triggers pandemonium in the stands as the locals join arms to celebrate the unlikely rescue mission. There's cheering and hugs, arm waving and shouting. Then the referee's whistle is blown. But it's not the final blast of the game. It's another penalty… for Shirebrook.

The howls of celebration turn to silence as Kyle Lilley steps up to score. The pocket of visiting fans are now the ones in dreamland, as the sound of slumped home supporters slipping back into their seats can be heard. To make matters worse, away manager Russ Eagle wheels down the touchline, à la Jose Mourinho's pitch-side charge at Old Trafford back in his Porto days.

The Loughborough faithful may be deflated, but the players aren't throwing in the towel yet. There's time for one last attack and as a long ball is arrowed into the box, Shirebrook fail to clear and it presents itself for Dasaolu to head home at the far post.

It's the fourth goal in 12 incredible minutes and the stand erupts again. Dasaolu, quite aptly, launches into a supersonic sprint down the touchline as his teammates try to catch their hero.

There will be no early exit this time, at least not today. Loughborough's

FA Cup dream is still alive and kicking.

Three days later, Loughborough's coach pulls up to Shirebrook's Langwith Road, with the team hoping to start in the same vein as they finished on Saturday.

The 2,000-capacity ground couldn't be much further away from the plush surroundings at Loughborough University Stadium. For all the modern sports facilities that greet the students for a home game, the only evidence of any other competition taking place in this patch of Derbyshire is what appears to be a roped-off greyhound track that runs down a straight for roughly 100 metres.

Inside the ground, the facilities continue to contrast with what the two sides played on at the weekend. The partially scorched grass on the pitch appears to have seen better days and a pair of matching iron stands provide the seating. It's a tidy ground for the 10th tier of English football, but a stark reminder to all of Loughborough's newcomers that they're playing in non-league.

In front of fewer than 100 fans, the Scholars look much more comfortable from the outset. Avoiding the defensive struggles that blighted them on Saturday, the students soon take control, with goals by Trotman, Matthew Crookes and Dasaolu sealing a comfortable 3-0 win that sends the Scholars into the next preliminary round.

The prize is a home tie against Northern Premier League side Gresley. And it proves to be where Loughborough's cup run ends – one round away from equalling their best performance in the FA Cup.

The Scholars went into the match against the higher league Moatmen unbeaten – following a win and another high-scoring draw in their opening two league fixtures. After a promising first half that saw Tom Barnes help Loughborough to a 1-1 scoreline, the game changed in stoppage time when Brenan was sent off for a second bookable offence. The red card spelled the end for the hosts, with two goals from Gresley's Tendai Chitiza and another from Ben Harris putting the result beyond doubt. A 4-1 defeat and yet more FA Cup disappointment for the boys in purple. But as the players traipsed off the pitch at the final whistle, one fan offers some consolation from the towering main stand: "Keep your heads up, lads. There's always next year!"

It's a token of perspective that becomes even more relevant as the month progresses.

RIP DANNY

The news came out of the blue. As Skubala listlessly scrolled through the Twitter feed on his phone, he stopped. His eyes locked on the screen, frozen. A feeling of anxiety and fear spread through his body as he read the message again. He still couldn't believe what he was seeing.

Danny Wilkinson, a former Loughborough University player who had only graduated that summer, had collapsed on the pitch during an Integro Doodson League Cup match between Shaw Lane Aquaforce and Brighouse Town. The 24-year-old had gone down with a suspected cardiac arrest after an hour of the tie and had been rushed to hospital. The news had spread like wildfire on social media, as the country's football fraternity prayed for his recovery.

Skubala couldn't believe it. Wilkinson had only completed his degree months earlier and was well-known to Skubala and many of the current squad, having turned out for the Scholars before moving back to his home county of Yorkshire to live with his girlfriend.

Loughborough's football programme had done its job. Wilkinson had signed up in 2012, following a stint in Hull City's youth team, and turned to further education to forge a new career path. Just as many others had done previously, Wilkinson combined studying for his degree in accounting and financial management with keeping his passion for football alive. He'd been a success. Over the four years he was part of the Loughborough set-up, Wilkinson had pulled on the university's purple shirt in both the BUCS and Midland Football League teams, forming an integral part of both sides.

When Wilkinson arrived, he was one of few youngsters who already had experience of non-league football, having been loaned out to Harrogate Town and North Ferriby United during his time at Hull. Football was his passion and it was clear that he'd be an asset to the university.

Now, on just another night that would have started with Wilkinson running out on the pitch ready for action, he lay motionless for half an hour as paramedics desperately administered CPR to get his heart beating again. An ambulance had taken him to Calderdale Royal Hospital in Halifax where doctors were working to save his life.

And there was Skubala, helplessly staring at his phone, trying to digest what was happening to a former player 100 miles north – just as countless other teammates, opponents and fans who knew Wilkinson would be doing all over the country. All that could be done was to hope for a positive update on his condition.

As news of Wilkinson's collapse spread on the Tuesday morning after the incident, a short statement on Shaw Lane's website from their chairman, Craig Wood, revealed the worst:

'It's with great sadness that we have to announce the tragic loss of Daniel Wilkinson, who has sadly passed away after collapsing on the pitch during the game last night. Our thoughts and prayers are with his family and friends at this time. The club would like to thank everyone for their heartfelt messages and thoughts that we have received throughout the night. There are no more words at this time.'

Only, there were plenty of words. Disbelief, sadness, despair. Wilkinson was only doing what he loved and would never have thought that the match at Brighouse would be the final action of his young life. With his family, girlfriend and Shaw Lane teammates around him, Wilkinson had been pronounced dead at the hospital.

It emerged that he had an underlying heart condition, Arrhythmogenic Right Ventricular Cardiomyopathy (ARVC), which had lain previously undetected. The rare disease affected Wilkinson's heart muscle, which left the ventricle thin and stretched, meaning blood wasn't being pumped around his body properly.

As Shaw Lane's statement reverberated around the football world and the nation's media outlets picked up on the tragedy, condolences flooded in. Words of support were sent from the FA, a whole manner of clubs and people who knew Wilkinson.

Loughborough followed suit and Skubala drafted a statement to appear on the university football website. It was simple and heartfelt:

'Our thoughts are with Danny's family and friends at this difficult time. After graduating from Loughborough University this summer, Danny had just embarked upon the next chapter in his life, and will be sadly missed by current and former members of our football family.

'Danny was both an accomplished student and footballer, who had a great life ahead of him. A young man with great character and liked by all, Danny had a positive influence on everyone he met at Loughborough and will be sorely missed by those who knew him best.'

By now, all of the players would know. In a world where news is available at the swipe of a screen, there was no way to break it to the players other than to let them find out by text, on social media or by browsing the latest football news.

The players were due to meet later that afternoon ahead of an evening fixture away at Sporting Khalsa on the outskirts of Birmingham. It would be a tricky match under the best of circumstances, but now it felt like an impossible ask for a team of young men, most of who were mourning the loss of a friend. Skubala called Brennan and the duo agreed to offer to call the match off, regardless of any possible FA recriminations for taking the action without prior permission. They'd take a points deduction or a fine if it meant protecting their players from a gut-wrenching coach trip and contest when they'd prefer to be alone with their thoughts. It would be the players' choice to play or not.

One by one, the players arrived at the agreed time for the match. Some of their faces told the story of their loss: distraught at the thought of having lost somebody who would so often have been with them as they prepared for an away trip like this. Five or six of the lads were crying and the players who had never met Wilkinson were evidently shaken.

As Skubala and Brennan began to explain that there was no pressure on the players to make the trip to Sporting Khalsa, the mood changed. The players wanted to get on the coach. They wanted to come together in the dressing room and play. They wanted to honour Wilkinson by going out there and playing the sport he died doing.

There was no way that any of the players were going to let the match be postponed, and nobody was going to let the news stop them from playing. So the grieving squad boarded an understandably subdued coach to make the journey to Willenhall to play only hours after their friend had passed away.

OOOO

When I arrived at Sporting Khalsa's Aspray Arena, I didn't know what to expect. I'd been following the news and updates throughout the day but hadn't realised quite how close the match had been to being called off.

As I pulled up alongside a floodlit five-a-side pitch that sat next to the ground, I called Mat to meet him at the turnstile. After greeting me with his customary handshake and warm smile, he turned to me and said: "Have you heard the news?"

We discussed the day's events as we wandered into the ground and he told me that many of the players, in particular captain Danny Brenan, had been serious doubts for the match right up until the teamsheets were filled in. Despite their brave attempts to carry on, were the players in the right mindset to play?

Brenan was one of a handful of this season's squad who had been particularly close to Wilkinson and they were all visibly emotional, even as they got changed in the dressing room. There'd been tears throughout the afternoon, but nobody would accept that they couldn't make it out there.

As I moved around to the corner of the ground, a strange misty gloom clung to the stands. It was only September but the thick haze was creating a hold that enveloped everything inside it – almost like the compact stadium had created its own micro-climate. In many ways, the conditions mirrored how many of the players must have been feeling. For all of the terrible thoughts that were going through their minds, they had to focus on what would happen on the pitch, if only for 90 minutes. The rest of the world could wait.

Settling in a seat that nestled among the steep steps of the ground's main stand, I watched the grey fog wrap an atmospheric backdrop around the occasion. By the time the two teams emerged for the minute's silence, any semblance of a skyline had been erased.

Loughborough's players linked arms around the centre circle and united in an eerie hush that engulfed the ground. If you watch closely enough during any minute's silence at a football match or sporting event, you can normally spot one or two players whose minds are drifting to the contest ahead. But not tonight. Heads bowed and eyes closed or staring forward, Loughborough's row of comrades felt every second of the silence. Only 24 hours earlier, Wilkinson had lined up ready for kick-off in a match he wouldn't finish – a humbling thought for every player on the pitch to consider.

If there had been any lingering doubts about whether Brenan was in a fit state to play, there was a resounding answer within the opening minutes.

Khalsa breaks out of defence quickly, releasing striker Luke Shearer in the area. He's got a few yards on his marker, but shortly before unleashing an effort at goal, Brenan leaves the ground to make the tackle. The gangly defender is at his limit as he slides, outstretched, towards Shearer's feet to gobble up the chance. But the forward loses his footing and yells in protest as Brenan's toe connects with the ball in perfect time to scoop it away from goal. The hosts' bench joins in with Shearer's appeal, but the referee dismisses any claim for a penalty. It's a brilliant tackle.

Brenan's challenge is the epitome of Loughborough's opening to the match, as they chase after every ball and provide a strong barrier against a gnarly and experienced Sporting outfit, who'd earned plaudits for an unlikely FA Cup run last year and were among the favourites to get promotion this season. They're tough and hard to beat, but Loughborough are up to the battle.

The Scholars' resilience is already starting to irk the hosts, with every challenge and decision met with a cry of injustice from a home player, coach or fan. And the pressure is starting to tell. Joe Jackson's timing is only slightly out as he jostles for the ball in the area, but the referee rules it as a trip and Dave Meese converts the resulting penalty to give Khalsa the lead.

It's a night for resilience and character, an occasion that you could forgive the students for letting get on top of them after the setback. But they won't roll over, not today. They begin to rally, with Alex Read forcing Tom Turner into a diving save down to his right, then Elliott Legg hitting a sighter from the edge of the area that fizzes only inches over the bar.

Just as it looks as though the visitors are about to strike, the game turns. O'Keefe takes one touch too many before clearing on the edge of his box and his hoof forward is charged down by Danny Ashton. The forward's on an angle, but he must surely roll the ball into the empty net.

Not if O'Keefe can help it. He lunges into Ashton and clatters him to the ground, after nicking the ball from his foot. It's a foul and a straight red for O'Keefe: the goalkeeper sinking back on to his haunches with his head in his hands before traipsing across the pitch to the dugout. The youngster is clearly upset and seeks out Brennan on his way past, apologising to his manager before trudging off. O'Keefe can barely stand to look at the rest of his bench on his way to the dressing room. The one place he doesn't want to be on his own.

Even with more than half of the game to play with only 10 men, Loughborough continue to scrap and are more than a match for Sporting, with only Marvin Nisbett's header exerting O'Keefe's replacement, James Stallan, for much of the second half.

The Scholars are gritty and well-organised, not giving their opponents an inch. And they nearly get their reward when Drew Bridge's dipping cross almost catches Turner out at the other end.

With time running out, Khalsa are up in arms again over another refereeing decision. A looping cross from the left is flicked past Stallan by Ashton and appears to have crossed the line at the far post, but is hacked away before the linesman can give it.

While the home dugout erupts in a barrage of abuse directed at the officials, Loughborough launch a counter attack. When Matthew Crookes' parried effort falls into Legg's path, the industrious midfielder can do nothing more than tap the rebound into the net.

The students jump up and celebrate the goal. It's everything they've deserved for their efforts and is a release of rare delirium in a day of unimaginable downs. Their emotion and togetherness is on full display as the team come together to celebrate.

Legg's goal won't be enough to earn a point though. In the closing stages, Bekir Halil tees up Meese, whose header agonisingly creeps past Stallan's reach to give Khalsa a 2-1 win and all three points. But the result doesn't matter, it's the manner of the performance that stands out and what it represents. As the players come off the pitch at full-time, they can hold their heads high.

Whether it was escapism or the freedom of crossing that white line on to the pitch, the players had done themselves proud. It was one of the best performances of the season so far, thanks to the hardy spirit resonating through the squad. This is why they refused to let Skubala call off the match. It was about channelling the sadness that poured out of them and doing something in Wilkinson's memory. Loughborough's students had done it in his honour.

RIP Danny.

THE SECOND COMING

Pre-season in September is a new one for me. So when a message popped up in my email inbox from Mat's football coordinator email address with details of a pre-season training schedule, I was left peering at my calendar in confusion.

It had been a month and a half since Loughborough started their campaign on that sunny Saturday afternoon against Shirebrook and they'd been playing two matches a week ever since.

In fact, the concern that greeted the season opener had long since been forgotten. Other than their FA Cup exit at the hands of higher-league Gresley, this year's students had only lost two further fixtures and were sitting comfortably in the top half of the Midland Premier League. It's a far cry from this stage of the previous year when the Scholars were languishing at the bottom of the table without a single point to their name.

So as I scanned through the training schedule that had been sent to the performance squad at the beginning of September, I wondered what the players could possibly have done to warrant a second pre-season. It's the time of year that most players dread, so to go through it twice in quick succession seemed harsh.

The carefully planned grid of activities attached to the email told me there was to be a series of conditioning sessions in and outside of the gym, and optional talks to go over Loughborough's approach for the season ahead. Friendly matches against Championship neighbours Burton Albion and Conference North outfit Nuneaton Town rounded off the two-week schedule.

"The second pre-season isn't for all of the players," Mat tells me when I next see him, towards the end of the training block. "The idea is mainly to get the new starters or the lads who didn't get to do a full pre-season before August up to speed, but some of the players from the first team will join in too.

"The trials for new players have happened since the start of the season too, so we brought in a few of the better ones before the training started. There are a handful of other players we haven't had the chance to see in proper games or who have been away over the summer and need match fitness."

Hundreds of hopeful young footballers went along to the university trials that were held at the Holywell pitches that sit opposite the stadium. Over a number of sessions, the lush green fields were flooded with a collection of freshers and older students, hoping to earn a coveted spot in one of Loughborough's fabled squads.

For the more ambitious players, their prospective prize lay tantalisingly close. Quite literally. Loughborough University Stadium sits at the top of the Holywell complex, peeking over a row of trees and a newly gravelled footbridge on to the row of outside pitches. Yet the trials will have been the closest most of the young men will ever get to playing in the stadium.

The lads with the most potential were monitored by Skubala and his team of coaches to decide which were good enough to go further, with the best players offered a chance to join the performance group that fly the flag in the Midland Premier League and BUCS Premier North.

A total of 33 players made it into the initial squad registered for first-team competition, although some may still fall by the wayside over the coming weeks. The rest of the hopefuls are either divided into the supporting squads for the Wednesday afternoon BUCS leagues or left to play in the weekly intramural or social competitions that take place on the campus's all-weather pitches.

It's not always as straightforward as picking the best players though. After adjusting to university life, some of those selected decide that the commitment required to be part of Loughborough's elite isn't for them. And the appeal of student life and a thriving social scene has more of a draw than an endless series of training sets throughout the season. Only the most dedicated will stay and it's that natural selection process, which weans out the players who aren't mentally prepared for the life of a student sportsman, that provides an informal second trial.

One of the players who has always had his eyes firmly focused on making the final squad is foreign exchange student Christoph Ivanusch. A 19-year-old Austrian who is at Loughborough on a year-long Erasmus course to study political science, Ivanusch was part of the reserve side at his local club Wacker Innsbruck before moving to Britain.

Although he arrived in England in late July, Ivanusch has faced an excruciating wait on the sidelines for the chance to pull on a Loughborough shirt as it took six weeks for his registration to be transferred from Wacker. When, on the eve of the second pre-season, he received permission to play, it was finally time for him to show what he could do.

I'd sat with Ivanusch in the stands at several matches in the first month of the season and he spoke passionately about his love for the game and how he'd been attracted to Loughborough by the university's top sports facilities. While his degree is most important, the youngster was keen to find somewhere that would allow him to take his football career seriously too. And the appeal of coming to England for a year was an opportunity he couldn't ignore.

"I've always hated the rain, so my mum was telling me that I was coming to the wrong country," he jokingly told me during one of the times we sat together.

"I've always wanted to live in England, so I looked at how I could come over here. When I saw that one of my options was to come to Loughborough and join the football programme, I was very excited – there is nothing like this in Austria.

"I'd never heard about Loughborough before I looked at the exchange programme, but when I saw it, I knew it was what I wanted. I was living at home with my parents, so this is a big move for me. Football is very important to me and I want to improve here."

Kitted out in a Liverpool tracksuit top, Ivanusch's knowledge of English football astounded me as we spoke in great detail about Jurgen Klopp and Premier League seasons gone by. As we sat, chatting away while watching Loughborough's matches, I got the impression that he was grateful for the company.

As an international student, Ivanusch had been placed in halls with others from around the globe. So when he arrived several weeks before term started, he found himself living with scores of Chinese students. They were in England on a summer coaching course, learning about the English game, and getting qualifications in sports psychology and performance analysis. While the Asian contingent had been friendly, the language barrier made socialising difficult. Ivanusch's English was excellent, but his command of Mandarin needed some work.

After taking several long walks to get his bearings around the campus, the young Austrian found that Loughborough's matches took on an even greater significance. He travelled home and away to watch the team play, and attended all of the squad's training sessions to get himself in shape for when his registration was finally rubber-stamped. He'd also admitted that the distraction of the Olympic Games – despite his Austrian countrymen's struggles to claim a medal of any colour – and regular visits to the gym had helped him through the opening weeks of his English experience before the rest of the permanent students arrived.

After spending a lot of time discussing his hopes as he longingly watched from the stands, I don't mind admitting that I was rooting for Ivanusch to do well when I finally got to see him in action in the friendly against Nuneaton.

Arriving at the same Holywell pitch where the trials had been held only days earlier, I scan the players in the starting line-up to see if he's out there, but to no avail. As I wander around to take my place on the grassy bank that surrounds the football field playing host to tonight's match, I spot Ivanusch sitting on the bench.

It's frustrating to see but, after weeks of waiting for the green light to play, waiting an hour or so to get out on the pitch must feel like child's play for Ivanusch. And after a first 45 minutes of loosening up along the touchline and sitting patiently on the sheltered substitutes' bench, he's finally given the signal to come on at half-time.

Ivanusch had always talked about being a central defender in Austria, so I was surprised to see him employed as a defensive midfielder when he came on in the second half of the match. And, in truth, it isn't the greatest of displays.

Nuneaton, who play three divisions above, are a professional outfit and are too good for Loughborough's students – athletic striker David Moli, in particular, getting a lot of joy against Ivanusch and co. The exchange student looks relatively small on the pitch alongside some of his opponents and he's left wanting as Moli shows his searing pace to streak past him on a couple of occasions.

What does impress me is Ivanusch's reading of the game. Not surprisingly, considering his insightful analysis from the stands, he has a deliberate knack of anticipating what will happen before play develops. Non-league might still be a bit of a culture shock for the young European, but Ivanusch's natural understanding of the game will surely serve him well throughout the campaign.

"English football is quite different to what I'm used to in Austria – I'm enjoying it though," Ivanusch tells me after the match.

"It's a lot more aggressive here than in Austria, where it's a lot more possession-based. My first game was against Burton a few days ago, when I played at centre back, but I have moved into central midfield since then.

"English football seems to be more about hitting the big man and putting the fast players in – it's much more direct than I'm used to. It's interesting and I have to learn a lot and need to get into my head that the style is to get the ball forward as quickly as possible to find a gap in the defence.

"We have to think forward. The first thing you should look at here is playing quickly and that's the main difference. I think I'm a better player already and I've learned a lot – I've improved physically too."

It's fascinating to think that, even in the lower leagues, the difference in playing styles between England and other European nations is so blindingly obvious to a visiting player, even though the Loughborough ethos is to play a brand of football that develops students technically as well as physically. It's not all about winning, but the need for points can't be ignored.

"I want to improve here and maybe see if there's a chance to play at a higher level in the future," Ivanusch continues. "My ambition is to get the best out of me, but my dream – just like any other footballer – is to play for a big club professionally one day. It's a big dream and very far away, but maybe it's possible. There's a long, long way to go though.

"I'm not thinking too much about what's coming up in June when I am meant to go back to Austria. At the moment, I plan to go back and will look to join a new club in the fourth division or something, but maybe something else will come up before that."

Having come from a professional club in Austria and with plans to move back after his year-long exchange comes to an end, it makes me wonder how much Ivanusch can take away that will be applicable for football on the continent. He's not the only international student who has joined up with the Scholars' performance squad – German teenager Manuchim Oke-William has also crossed the English Channel to play, despite having experience at TSV 1860 Munich in his homeland.

Loughborough's football programme clearly has a wide appeal. Even within the squad of 20-odd players that took to the field against Nuneaton, there's an array of different personalities and backgrounds.

While some of the lads have come here solely for the education and found their way into the first team, there are a host of academy drop-outs too. Luke Trotman, he of the missed penalty in the FA Cup game against Shirebrook, enrolled at uni after being released by Luton Town, while there are also former youth teamers from a scattering of other Football League clubs, including Gillingham and Oldham Athletic. For them, Loughborough's football programme provides the perfect safety net when their dreams of reaching the big time hit the ropes. By turning to education, the players receive a solid grounding for a career away from the pitch, as well as the chance to develop in a professional environment on it.

While Britain's university football teams aren't teeming with talent like some sports in the US, where college competition provides a well-trodden path to stardom, there are a number of current professionals who have successfully made the transition from student loans to a full-time contract.

Sunderland winger Duncan Watmore graduated with a first-class honours degree in economics and business management around the same time he broke into the Black Cats' first team. He even transferred from Manchester to Newcastle University when he moved to the north-east. Then there's Huddersfield forward Joe Lolley, who earned a move to the Football League straight from higher education.

Loughborough don't offer scholarships for players to join their football programme and don't even pay travel expenses to players who turn out for the non-league side, but they do look for possible candidates from the nation's academies who might benefit from the university experience. And sometimes it's not the step down it might initially seem.

"At Luton, it's all about getting the three points on a Saturday, whereas here the club cares about you as a person," says former Hatter, Trotman, who turned to education after being released in May.

"I didn't get another contract at Luton after being a first-year pro and could have gone to a non-league club near me, but I thought this was a better option because I can get a degree and still play football at a decent level."

While a lot of former academy pros find themselves on the scrap heap with little idea of how to turn their ailing careers around at such a young age, Trotman is one of the lucky ones. He'd applied through UCAS to come to Loughborough before he received the news that he wouldn't be getting a new contract. After a lot of soul searching, Trotman decided that getting a degree was the wisest move, although he admits making it as a professional footballer is still his number-one ambition.

"The length of a degree is a long time to be out of the professional game and it's daunting," he adds. "But because the set-up is good here, it's similar to being at a football club. Coming here is more of a long-term thing and my plan is to go back into full-time football afterwards, with a degree. It has happened before, so hopefully it'll happen again with me."

Most recently, former Loughborough captain George Williams has made his way back to the Football League after opting for a stint at university. He won promotion to the Championship with Barnsley before moving back to MK Dons, where he had been a trainee. He's not the only one either, with other alumni including ex-Charlton midfielder Bradley Pritchard and Exeter City's Robbie Simpson, using education as a route back to the top.

While coming from a professional academy might improve a player's chances of using Loughborough as a stepping stone to greater things, an impressive-looking CV won't open doors at the university all on its own. Some applicants, like Trotman, might be marked out as promising talents before starting their degree, but they will all be treated in the same way when it comes to earning a place in the team. There is no special treatment in the Scholars squad, according to Skubala.

"It's a shock for players at first and we have a number of released players coming in," he says. "It's difficult because sometimes they have to see the harsh reality of football.

"In some big academies, some players are only kept there to help other players develop. It sounds harsh, but there could be one or two diamonds in, say, the Leicester City youth team and the others are there to make up the numbers. So when certain players are released, they're not one of the better players here – they have been kept on to progress others. So they'll arrive and not be as good as some of the others who haven't been at an academy.

"Some players get this label that they're better, but it's not always the case. Alternatively, you can really tell the players who have been at clubs where they've had first-team experience and then come to us. Sam Minehane, for example, was a great lad who has now gone on to Stockport County and there's Daniel Nti too, who is now at York City. They both came in to us at a high level.

"Compare that to an 18-year-old academy drop-out who has no first-team experience. They've maybe played 12 games a year and are suddenly thrust into 50 or 60 games a season. It can take them a bit of time: technically they can do it, but they don't have the real game bit yet."

It can be hard enough for teenagers to adapt to life away from home anyway, so adding in the stress of dealing with a demanding football environment can be tough. The support is there, but it is about give and take. And, importantly, the education is always given priority.

Whereas young sportsmen in the US are placed on college scholarships that revolve around their talent on the field, any promising players arriving at Loughborough without the necessary grades have to be turned away. Similarly, if their performance in the classroom drops, they'll risk losing their place in the team, regardless of how good they are.

As more and more football programmes pop up around the country, different models are available. Loughborough's education-first approach is backed up by offering no financial reward for playing in the non-league team, even though other local clubs in comparable leagues offer a match fee. Other unis try it differently, with sports scholarships offered to entice the best players into their football programme. However, Skubala insists Loughborough is unlikely to change any time soon.

"First and foremost, players are here to study and we're not afraid to tell them that," he tells me.

"When lads come here, they see the environment we've got with our stadium and that we're as professional as some teams in the Football League, but we need to make sure that they know why they're here. We have to manage expectations.

"Part of that is saying they're here for a reason and have a great opportunity to be creative, but they need to study first. Hopefully, with our support, some of the better characters and players can step up again, whether that's into the Conference or higher."

With all eyes on the players in the early weeks of their time here, the ambitious young footballers will need that combination of brains and talent to realise their potential. As I continue to immerse myself in Loughborough's world, I soon find out how one former player is seen to epitomise how making the right choices at such a youthful age can make all the difference.

BRADLEY'S HALFWAY HOUSE

Many people can't pinpoint the decision that changed their life forever. With the butterfly effect of fate subtly intertwined with every snap judgement and instinctive move we make, putting the onus on one key turning point is almost impossible.

Not so for Bradley Pritchard, who can trace the catalyst for his life's transformation back to an impulsive choice he made in the heart of Loughborough's thriving campus: one the teenager swore he'd never make when he first enrolled. But as many students find, peer pressure can be a persuasive mistress.

The former Charlton Athletic and Leyton Orient midfielder had vowed to turn his back on football altogether after he signed up to study for a degree in English and sports science back in 2005. It was to be a new start for the sport-mad fresher, as he changed his focus to hockey after suffering a series of painful rejections at Crystal Palace, Luton Town and Gillingham as a hopeful young prospect. Fed up with being beaten down by football's notorious ruthlessness, Pritchard saw hockey as promising a much brighter future. That's until one of his friends twisted his arm to go along to a second-team training session, catapulting him on to an unexpected trajectory that ended in the Football League.

"When I was growing up, I was always good at football and hockey, and I had to decide between one and the other," explains Pritchard, as he looks back at the moment that changed his life's direction forever.

"I ended up playing football at first but I'd become disillusioned with it so I decided to concentrate on hockey instead. I went to university without thinking of football as something I'd do there.

"I started playing hockey and one of the guys in my halls said 'if you were at Palace, then why don't you try out for the team?'. So I went to second-team training with him and was introduced to James [Ellis, then director of football] and I liked the way he worked.

"He told me to stay in and around the first team. Because I'd turned up late, I wasn't a starter for them and was more of a second-team player who turned out for the first team now and again."

So with the promise of more first-team appearances, Pritchard stuck around. And as his all-action displays continued to catch the eye, the midfielder soon found he was being called upon more and more.

Football's gain was hockey's loss. A naturally talented sportsman, who shone whether he had a ball at his feet or on the end of a hockey stick, Pritchard had seemed destined to play for one of British hockey's top clubs and had already taken part in international trials to play for England. But as Pritchard rediscovered his verve for football on Loughborough's training pitches, his hockey stick started to gather dust.

His U-turn didn't happen overnight though. Standing at five foot eight inches tall, the midfielder had always been told that he was too small to make it as a professional footballer and believed that doors would continue to be shut in his face due to his stature rather than his footwork.

While getting games for Loughborough's BUCS teams due to his quick feet and eye for a defence-splitting pass was good, it wasn't necessarily going to spell the beginning of another crack at the big time. Although the more Pritchard was exposed to the training methods of Ellis and Head

Coach Tom Curtis, the more he found that his initial preconceptions of university football didn't quite ring true.

"I'd always heard that university football was something you do with your mates and then get drunk afterwards. Whereas sports like hockey, cricket and rugby were more traditional routes for student athletes to go to a higher level," he says, with a wry smile at the irony.

"I thought that if you're playing with university football players, if they're any good, they should be playing pro. I thought you were never going to play football at a particularly good standard there, but Loughborough certainly changed my view."

Pritchard found that he wasn't the only footballer at Loughborough with a hard-luck story to tell. Plenty of other teenagers who had chosen the promise of education over the rejections and ruthless nature of the professional game had found their way to Loughborough, and he soon felt at home with a squad brimming with talent.

Whether these players had been turned away by clubs due to their size, ability or perceived lack of progress, Loughborough's squad was finally given the platform to flourish out on the pitch. They were allowed time to develop and with no money or big contracts around to create friction in the squad, the team were free to focus on improving as players and being successful.

When Pritchard started studying at Loughborough in 2005, the university didn't have a team in the Midland Football League. So after establishing himself as an important member of the first-team squad, he and several other players started spending their weekends playing for some of the region's non-league clubs.

Ellis, who was now coaching at Conference North outfit Nuneaton Town, took Pritchard to play for the Warwickshire club. And as the diminutive midfielder tells me about how he shared his time at either side of the county border, there's a real sense of what a happy time it was for him.

Gone are the subdued tones he used as he harked back to his disappointments as a teenager trying to earn professional contracts in the Football League. Instead, he talks excitedly as he recalls how he juggled his commitments challenging for promotion with Nuneaton and BUCS glory with Loughborough. Even now, more than a decade on, it is clear that his passion for the game was back.

"Going to Loughborough did rekindle that love for football because it was a perfect mix of training full-time, without the complication of money," Pritchard affirms.

"It was just guys who enjoyed playing football and were playing at a good level with fantastic facilities. We trained on pitches and in gyms of such a standard that isn't accessible to 70% of clubs in the Football League and training was all geared to enhancing you as a player.

"Ultimately, James knew that he was only going to have us for three years and then we'd move on, so while he wanted to achieve things, he instilled a very good ethos and focus on development. If we'd gone to any other university, I'm sure we wouldn't have been exposed to that sort of high-quality training so often.

"Loughborough gave us that buzz and because we were a successful team, it made us want to be more and more successful, which is ultimately why you play football in the first place."

That was certainly true for Pritchard. After two successful years at Nuneaton, which only ended when the club was liquidated and demoted two divisions, the Zimbabwe-born midfielder joined neighbours Tamworth. And while at The Lamb, he earned promotion to the Conference and got the chance to test himself against full-time opposition for the first time. It was his time in the Conference that got Pritchard noticed. After impressing with Tamworth, he moved back down south to Hayes & Yeading, before he got the offer he'd all but given up hope of receiving. Third tier Charlton Athletic were interested in taking him to The Valley, where at the age of 24, he would finally pen his first professional contract in the Football League.

Pritchard's first season with the Addicks ended just as his maiden campaign with Tamworth did – with promotion. This time, the league championship that took Charlton to the Championship marked an incredible ascent for Pritchard, just three years after graduating from university without a clear plan of where his next step would be.

"I would never have believed it when I was at uni," says Pritchard. "When you go to uni and you see a lot of young players being given debuts, it's almost as though you're giving up on the dream.

"What you're saying is: for the next three to four years, football isn't my priority. I'm not going to chase my dream because I'm going to get an education – and you can't do both things. When you choose to go to university, you're indirectly saying that it's not going to happen. To say I'll be a student, then to become a professional footballer at 24, it's not meant to work like that.

"It was quite late on when I got that pro offer from Charlton – I didn't expect to get that at that point. But when it came through, I said this was the dream and I wasn't going to turn it down."

Pritchard stayed at Charlton for three seasons and spent two more years at London neighbours Leyton Orient, before leaving full-time football at the end of the 2015/16 season to take a Legal Practice Course (LPC) as he aimed to find a new career in sports law.

Looking back at where his career was heading as a teenager who was receiving countless knock-backs from Football League clubs, Pritchard still struggles to believe that he ever made it as a professional. When he arrived at Loughborough as an 18-year-old, he'd lost his way and was prepared never to kick another ball in a competitive match.

"I was too young to cope with how ruthless an environment football is," he says. "When you see one or two youngsters who are given their debuts, it gives you a taste of what can be achieved and you really want that. But there's very little patience when it comes to player development.

"I thought a lot of football coaches had a mould of how players should be and you either fitted into it or were moved along. You do get a lot of players who leave the professional game because they can't see themselves fitting in.

"In the end, I just didn't want to play anymore because I was fed up of being rejected. Other players are a lot tougher and I think you have to be thick-skinned to play football, but I just thought 'I don't need this, I'm going to university' and my focus changed.

"For my own personal wellbeing, I had to step away from professional football when I was 18 to try to discover what really excited me and what I wanted from life – I hadn't found it before then. Loughborough helped to put things into perspective. For a football player who was a bit disillusioned, it was the perfect halfway house."

Just before we go our separate ways, I have one last question for Pritchard. While the now-31-year-old is doing just as he did when he was a student at Loughborough – combining studying with turning out for a part-time team, Isthmian Leaguers Greenwich Borough, four promotions below the Football League – does his latest career switch to the world of law mean he has turned his back on professional football for the final time?

"If I had one direction in life, I'd be happy," he admits, after letting out a knowing laugh. "But there are many things that keep coming my way.

"At the moment, I'm trying to finish my LPC, then I can apply for training contracts. The goal is to qualify and become a solicitor, but we'll see. With my background, I could definitely go back into football, whether as staff, in the boardroom or sporting law.

"From what I've seen in my career in the past 10 years, I never really know what's going to happen."

TWO GAMES, SIX HOURS

Jack Poxon has dé jà vu. As he jogs up and down the sparse touchline, changing direction at each marker, a familiar sensation washes over him. He's all too used to warming up ahead of a football match, but it's not the well-rehearsed preparation for kick-off that's the reason for the repetition that whirs around in the young student's mind. Well, not quite.

It's the second time in a matter of hours that Poxon has completed the drill. It's the second time in a matter of hours that Poxon is wearing the university's purple strip. It's the second time in a matter of hours that Poxon is playing a match for Loughborough. Looking around, Poxon can see a clutch of teammates who are going through the same scenario.

Less than six hours earlier, Poxon and the rest of the Scholars team were limbering up for the first of two matches that day. With the traditional Wednesday afternoon enrichment slot left free across the nation's universities for sporting competition, Loughborough faced a crunch BUCS Premier North fixture against the University of Stirling.

After making a winless start to the new BUCS league season, the clash with their Scottish counterparts was crucial to kick-start their campaign. This was the big match of the day and many of the squad's brighter lights were chosen to help get the much-needed three points, with a hotchpotch of other squad members left to play a Midland Football League Cup match later on. There were exceptions though. Some names appeared on both teamsheets as cover in either match, although their workloads would be managed to make sure that nobody was left playing too many minutes.

One of those names was Poxon, a final-year student who was on the books at Oldham Athletic before enrolling at Loughborough. He'd missed the first few weeks of the season while he completed a summer-long work placement at an investment bank in London, so maybe he was making up for lost time.

Poxon was a regular starter last season and was named on the bench as cover for the afternoon match against Stirling. But after falling behind to a goal after just five minutes, Loughborough's masterplan started to unravel.

The Scholars desperately chased the game, but couldn't find an equaliser, so turned to Poxon with half an hour left to play. And he was nearly the hero when his late free kick was beaten away by the Stirling goalkeeper. Despite a frantic finale, Loughborough's efforts were in vain and the players were left scratching their heads at how they'd lost the first of the day's matches 1-0. At least there was a chance to put it right in five hours' time.

With the hectic nature of non-league football regularly turning up two matches per week, it's not unusual for the Scholars' fixtures to stack up on Tuesday nights and Wednesday afternoons, particularly in the early months of the season. But when the League Cup put Loughborough up against Leicestershire neighbours Quorn on a Wednesday evening, the fixture list took on an even more congested look. The only saving grace was that the quaint village of Quorn sits only three miles away from Loughborough, so it was hardly a long slog to go from one match to the next.

As the autumnal sun was swallowed up by darkness, the team made the short trip to Quorn's Farley Way ground. Most of the players who played earlier in the day aren't involved in tonight's match, but many of them have travelled to support their teammates from the modest terraces that line the pitch.

There's a chill in the air as a steady stream of people enter the single block of turnstiles in the far corner of the ground. A congregation of familiar Loughborough faces have gathered by the gate that joins the pitch and the dressing rooms, with the hooded figure of Skubala in the middle. The performance manager cuts a downbeat figure, thanks to his side's defeat earlier on, and the weakened team that's printed in the clubhouse window near them suggests that in a couple of hours he might be dealing with a second successive blow. The players in the huddle seem frustrated too. No footballer enjoys watching his team play without them, even if they've only just completed 90 minutes, and there's a real sense that some of them would like to be in the starting XI to put things right.

"I prefer playing in the non-league matches, it's a bit more real," admits midfielder Elliott Legg, as the group breaks up to find a place to watch the match.

"It's like playing boys in BUCS and it's a bit more competitive when you play non-league. We've got to play in the game that's seen as the priority though."

Legg played earlier against Stirling and is one of those to have the night off. While he won't be having an impact on the Quorn pitch, he's offering his voice to the cause and is joined by captain Danny Brenan in giving left back Tom Rankin some stick as he runs up and down the touchline closest to them.

The duo are also amused by the sight of debutant Hafeez Sanusi, a strapping centre back who only signed up a few days earlier. Sanusi is a man-mountain at six-foot-four and has the appearance of a grizzled former pro almost 10 years their elder rather than a fellow university student – something Legg and Brenan are quick to point out from the stand. The centre back used to play for Grays Athletic and Billericay Town, so has been earmarked as the perfect fit to add some extra nous to the non-league team.

Another automatic pick is winger Jeremiah Dasaolu, who is no longer eligible to play for Loughborough in BUCS competition after failing his course and joining the local college instead. Other than that, the squad for the match was agreed between Skubala and Brennan at the start of the week. With wholesale changes throughout the team, it raises the question about how Loughborough's approach fits in with the FA's ruling to make sure clubs don't field weakened sides.

"Who's to say what our strongest team is?" Skubala smiles elusively when I mention this to him as he watches from a vantage point near the clubhouse. The performance manager was in the dugout for the BUCS game, but has deferred to Brennan for this evening.

"Nowhere is there a written rule that you need to play your strongest team. Coaches pick their strongest team on the day depending on the circumstances. And after all, my strongest player isn't always the same as Karl's, so how can you dictate that?"

The topic of best line-ups is particularly relevant when it comes to fixture clashes like this week. It normally calls for a meeting of the minds between Skubala and Brennan to figure out which players are most suitable for each match, with the final decision normally leaving one side weaker than the other, despite the intention of giving Loughborough the best chance of emerging victorious from both games.

While Skubala is theoretically Brennan's superior, he's not immune to criticism from the hierarchy above him if Loughborough's proud reputation is at risk of being damaged by poor performances. Hence why BUCS competitions normally get the nod, especially when the side is languishing at the bottom of the table with no win from three matches.

"We both like different players and some suit one competition more than others, so it normally works itself out pretty well," Skubala continues.

"At least we've been able to overlap with some of the lads today. We've had weeks in previous years when we've played a Midland Premier game on a Tuesday night and then been away in Scotland on the Wednesday afternoon.

"Karl understands what it's like at Loughborough, so is really good with that. Like the rest of us, he knows that we can't risk getting relegated from the BUCS Premier so that had to be the priority today. Losing earlier was bad for us and if we get knocked out here, it will be a terrible day all round."

An even start gives no early indication of whether that dreaded situation will occur. Dasaolu, whose form has dipped since his rip-roaring display on the opening day, goes close first with a deflected effort that's turned round for a corner.

Then Joe Jackson, another of the side who featured in the Stirling match, fires a left-footed volley straight at the goalkeeper from close range. Quorn have their chances too, most notably a Nathan Dale free kick that is held on to by Conor O'Keefe.

Then, disaster strikes. Midway through the second half, O'Keefe rushes a drop kick and gifts the ball to the hosts in a dangerous position. Loughborough's backline desperately scrambles back to retrieve the situation and Sanusi launches his colossal frame towards the ball, but overcommits. Winger Nick Goold is left in yards of space just inside the area and he steers a left-footed drive beyond a distraught O'Keefe and into the net.

Loughborough are 1-0 down for the second time today.

○○○○

Shortly before the midweek squad lists are revealed to the players, Brennan sends a text to his assistant. The message to Ricky Nurse contains the names of the players who will be in the squad for the Midland Premier League fixture later that week. Sometimes, Brennan doesn't need to read the reply to know Nurse's reaction.

Life as a football manager can be difficult at the best of times. But when your squad is like a revolving door from Saturday to midweek, with different names playing just days apart, the task becomes even harder. So with BUCS taking priority over the Midland Premier League competitions, Brennan and Nurse have to face up to the reality of being left with a shadow team on several occasions. And preparations undoubtedly suffer.

"It's a definite challenge," laments Brennan. "You can have up to 30 different players available to play each week when you've got to put the two squads together, which can end up diluting what you have to work with.

"It can be difficult to maintain a team's collectiveness or spirit, which is something the teams we're coming up against have all got. You do lose something when the lads are looking around the dressing room and the faces they're seeing are different."

While Brennan took the role last season under no illusions that there would be split priorities throughout the year, the reality is frustrating. As a spectator, I regularly find myself checking the teamsheet to see a smattering of unfamiliar names staring back at me, so it's no surprise that the upheaval is having an impact on performances too.

After a promising start to the campaign, inconsistency has crept into more than just the team selections. From a settled side in the early weeks of the season that looked capable of finishing in the division's top five, form has dipped and a series of indifferent results have left Loughborough heading for mid-table.

As a PE lecturer at Loughborough, Brennan understands the importance of protecting the university's reputation in BUCS competition. But as a manager hired to stand on the touchline and get results in a competitive division, the internal conflict of wanting the best for your charges rages on.

It takes a certain type of character to pour hours of time and effort into managing a club where you will probably have the core of your starting XI stripped away week after week, regardless of how well they're doing elsewhere for the university.

"I don't see how the lads can be developing and progressing if they're not winning. For me, they come together," says Brennan.

"Winning breeds confidence and better performances, so the frustration I feel is for the players because they go into some games they should win and don't. The biggest challenge is taking the culture with us and the hard work we did in pre-season – pulling the lads together, having a common goal and understanding each other's roles. That can all get a little bit lost when players are landing in different places.

"The ideal for me is that these lads go through an education that means they can turn up to any game in any context against any opponent and adapt, whether we turn up in the middle of Birmingham on a Tuesday night in the MFL or on a Wednesday in BUCS."

Supping on a bottle of beer, Brennan is refreshingly honest about the pitfalls of the job. We're catching up in the corner of a busy clubhouse with the hubbub of players and fans buzzing around us, and his eyes regularly dart away from our conversation whenever we cross a potentially contentious issue or discuss an example that involves one of his team.

Brennan is respectful in his answers but is open enough to explain the truth behind the politics that govern certain decisions. He's effusive in his praise of Loughborough's football programme and the university's excellent facilities, but admits it can still be tough to take when the club's busy fixture list stifles the progress that could be achieved on the pitch.

While it's Brennan's first managerial job in senior football, he's familiar with what it takes to be successful. Formerly on the books at Leicester City, Brennan played locally in non-league before taking on a series of coaching roles and becoming assistant manager at Quorn. But shortly after taking up a teaching position at Loughborough last year, he saw the manager's position for the university's Midland Premier League side advertised – and got the job. Not before asking questions about how it all worked though.

"So, if you don't mind me asking, how can you get sacked from a position like this?" I ask cheekily, fearing the response I might get. Luckily, Brennan takes it in good humour.

"If nobody knows, then let's not try to find out!" he laughs. "In truth, when I came to interview, that was one of the things I asked, but in a more positive way. I asked about what success looks like in the role and how I can do my bit. And last year that was to change the culture and philosophy to help players be more effective as students so they can get the careers they want.

"Me coming here isn't just about getting the strongest XI to play the best football they can – that's only part of it. It's also about helping young sports science interns like Jack Milligan, who is now at Leicester City, and young coaches like Alex Ackerley, who is bouncing between the

BUCS and MFL team, to build a CV so they can go on from here.

"I want to be a constant and want to keep developing as a coach myself, but I also want to help others around me to go on and infiltrate the game."

It's at this point that I begin to see the stark similarities between Brennan and Skubala. They're both hungry for success, but their thirst for victory doesn't come at all costs: they appear to care about the players' futures as much as the three points. It's hard to imagine many other football managers taking the same attitude.

The clandestine squad selections the pair hold every Monday when there's a midweek game might well be more heated than either let on, but I'm not about to receive an invite to show me their innermost secrets. Brennan compares the discussion to the legendary Anfield boot room, where Liverpool's great and good came together for decades to come up with a steadfast plan for victory. The only difference is that the Liverpool hierarchy never had to pick between playing John Barnes in a match on a Tuesday night or a Wednesday afternoon.

The only titbit I am given is that Brennan and Skubala are still trying to land on the best way to balance priorities. They want to win on all fronts, but so far, it's proving to be a much harder nut to crack than they thought.

"It's not that what we're doing isn't working, but we can always strive to do things better," concedes Brennan.

"We've talked about splitting groups of players for periods of time, rather than having no idea which players we'll have from a Tuesday to Saturday. That way, you'll know you'll have that group of lads for a fixed period of time. Then, for whatever reason, the next period of time may change.

"There are going to be idiosyncrasies and swaps, like injuries and illness, that dilute the pool but at the moment, we've chosen to pull off players in some games to protect them for another one. That's football and that's life. The biggest challenge at the moment is having a pool of players that is big enough and of sufficient quality to compete on two fronts."

OOOO

Quality appears to be the main concern at Quorn. While there's no shortage of commitment, the students are struggling to threaten the home side's goal and they're facing the prospect of falling to Loughborough's second defeat in just six hours.

Brennan and Nurse stand on the edge of their technical area watching as the students are thwarted again as they try to get an equaliser that will at least force extra time and 30 more minutes of football.

If picking two different line-ups for matches wasn't already putting enough strain on the squad, the subs' bench looks even more threadbare. With one of the five named replacements, Legg, sitting in the stands and backup goalkeeper Danny Wright the only other player available with much experience at this level, Brennan is hamstrung. He rubs his face with his right hand as he tries to conjure up a change that will give his side the extra impetus they need.

Brennan has just one wild card left and he's about to put him on. Forward Joe Boachie was meant to be part of the squad that played Stirling, but missed the match after mistakenly thinking he had been picked in the side for Quorn instead. His confusion cost him a place in either line-up but as Brennan gives him the signal, Boachie springs to his feet in preparation. As he gets his fresh legs stretched off ready for his one-man rescue mission, fatigue is showing on the pitch, with the hosts coming within inches of doubling their lead. The ball makes its way out to goalscorer Goold on the left again, but luckily for Loughborough, his shot rattles into the side netting.

It's the let-off Loughborough need and Boachie's emergence from the dugout does just the trick. But it's not the player getting his first minutes of the day that grabs the goal, it's the tired legs of Poxon instead.

The full back, who has now surpassed 100 minutes of football today, canters forward down the right flank and arrives on the edge of the area just in time to strike a piledriver beyond Leighton Smith in the Quorn goal. It's 1-1. Loughborough's fan club of players celebrate as Poxon signals to the bench that he's injured and will have to end his football marathon with the goal.

Despite the setback, the Scholars are in the ascendancy. A quick interchange on the edge of the area releases Christian Enerenadu, but he's tripped before he's able to pull the trigger. Penalty.

In the absence of some of the more regular penalty takers, Dasaolu picks up the ball. Having netted a wonderful individual goal against Alvechurch in the league the previous weekend, the spot kick is the winger's ticket to a second consecutive strike. The ground falls silent as he places the ball ahead of Smith and poises himself for the referee's whistle. As the shrill blast echoes all around, Dasaolu strikes the ball cleanly and true, and it rockets past Smith. But instead of turning to celebrate, the striker sinks to his knees in despair as he sees his effort wallop off the top of the crossbar and sail into the row of trees behind the goal.

The penalty miss consigns the match to extra time and takes the students' double-header to an eye-watering 210 minutes of football. Surely, there's only one winner coming out of this – and it's Loughborough.

With time running out before a penalty shoot-out, a corner comes flying in towards Boachie, who belies his height by rising highest to head a firm header downwards and bouncing into the roof of the net. A mixture of excitement and relief fills the players, as they leap on top of the unlikely match winner: a man who wasn't even meant to be playing.

Brennan and Nurse celebrate among themselves on the bench. With the final whistle just a few minutes later, they've secured victory against the odds and will progress to the next round of the cup.

"I've played two matches in 24 hours before but never in one afternoon," says a hobbling Poxon, after he congratulates his teammates on getting through.

"It was extremely hard, but it was good that we got one of the results today. If I hadn't have pulled my groin a couple of minutes before I scored, I would probably have carried on – although I don't know if I'd have done the entire 120 minutes tonight.

"I knew I was going to be playing two matches today when my name was on the squad list for both, so it's been a long old day. It started at nine with lectures in the morning, a game in the afternoon and one in the evening, then I'm driving back to Manchester tonight because I'm flying to a stag do tomorrow."

Shuffling back to the dressing room, Poxon embodies the chaos that can accompany Loughborough's midweek schedule. At least today there's a happy ending.

Just as the players warm down and get ready to leave Quorn, there's further good news. Thanks to today's marathon effort, the next morning's scheduled gym session has been cancelled to give their bodies time to recover. Small mercies, eh?

FRIENDS REUNITED

The clink of pint glasses is a familiar sound in Loughborough University Stadium's bar on a match day and today is no different. As locals and parents wander in alongside visiting Heanor Town fans to get a pre-match tipple, they jostle at the bar to get the attention of the two staff who valiantly keep the steady flow of punters satisfied.

The regular pre-match discussions are happening all around the purple-daubed room, which spans the length of the entire seating area of Loughborough's main stand. There are the shared pleasantries of acquaintances catching up, interested bystanders who are casting an idle ear to the television that plays commentary from the day's lunchtime match and guests checking out the plush ground for the first time.

Among the throng of match-goers gathering in the Loughborough bar, a pocket of VIPs is assembling to little fanfare. That's because today's Midland Football League fixture is the focus of the university's football alumni day and a host of former students are here to cast their minds back several decades to remember times when they represented the university. With kick-off half an hour away, the ex-players gather next to one of the tall glass windows that looks out on to the main stand and the pitch below. These sort of luxuries weren't afforded back in the alumni's day, but it doesn't take the old friends much time to begin reminiscing about what it used to be like. For most, it still feels like only yesterday, but as the ever-evolving world of football is keen to point out, things and players have moved on at pace.

Pints in hand, the former teammates greet each other warmly. Some were in the same year and lived together during their time on campus, whereas others have formed strong bonds in the following years while discussing mutual experiences at events such as this. While only the most ardent supporters with the longest memories might recognise some of the faces chattering away with each other, there are several clues nearby that hint towards their presence.

The long room doubles as a conference space throughout the year and is frequently used for induction sessions to show freshers at the start of the season what the football programme offers. To welcome the alumni, the area's expanse has been used to proudly display some of the top-achieving footballers who have attended Loughborough over the years – most of who were never given the opportunity to represent the university in a competitive non-league match as the current crop of students are now.

Shirts of some of the more recent graduates, who have gone on to become professionals, hang from the walls, with Bradley Pritchard, George Williams and Robbie Simpson's surnames proudly displayed.

A presentation runs on a loop on the white projector screen to tell the story of the university, its achievements on the pitch and how some of its favourite sons have gone on to achieve greater things.

"What we're trying to do with the alumni is bring people together. Linking the current with the past," says Tim Crane, who is a major impetus behind Loughborough's football alumni group.

"The essence of the alumni is to create an informal, but smart, network that brings people together, whether that's for a beer, a job opportunity or to help a current student.

"If I can stand here with a guy who came to Loughborough in 1952 telling me about how he coached in Uganda and we get on like we were in the same year, it's a nice essence to have. Whether people are from the 50s, 70s, 90s or nowadays, everyone gets on."

In his forties, Crane is introduced to me by Mat, who has helped to arrange for the alumni day to take place. Crane is smartly dressed, with his grey-flecked hair perfectly swept into a side parting, and, most appropriately, has a purple Loughborough scarf wrapped around his neck, displaying his colours with pride.

Crane was a business student between 1989 and 1992, and turned out for Loughborough's first team for a number of years. While sport – namely football – was always his first love, his feet were never likely to win him a full-time playing career, despite him carving out a good reputation on the non-league scene in the north-west, playing for Stalybridge Celtic in the Conference. Instead, Crane went into sales, working for Proctor & Gamble and office interiors company TSK Group, while organising Loughborough University events and activities in his spare time. It's a passion that's unrelenting and is something he takes great pride in, largely thanks to his status as a second-generation alumni.

"My dad came to Loughborough in the late 50s and 60s and played for the football team too," Crane says proudly.

"In his time at Loughborough, he shared a room with Barry Hines, who famously wrote the book A Kestrel For a Knave, which was made into the film Kes. Barry played football with people including (ex-Arsenal and Scotland goalkeeper) Bob Wilson, (former Crewe Alexandra boss) Dario Gradi and Keith Blunt, who went on to manage Malmo.

"Barry was a good right back and had played for Yorkshire Schools. He was a committed Yorskhireman – straightforward, dour and straight-talking – and wasn't keen on literature when he roomed with my dad; he read comics instead. My dad eventually chucked him a book, Animal Farm. It transformed his approach to literature and, after two years' teaching, he released his first book and went on to become a professional writer. But he was one of those men that, if you speak to any of his peers such as Bob Wilson, people see as an effective right back first and an international bestselling author second."

It's clearly a well-rehearsed anecdote that encapsulates everything that the university represents. Throughout an engaging chat with Crane, he references the 'little pockets' of players and their stories several times.

While we've moved away from the main hub of the former students laughing and joking, Crane's utopia is clear to see. On first sight, you'd think they were all old classmates, regaling each other with cherished tales from their teens, despite there being years between their graduation days.

Crane is still excitedly chattering about the wealth of experience that has come through Loughborough's ranks and leads me over to a board packed with photographs of various shapes, sizes and colours. Pictures of successful Loughborough University line-ups from across the decades.

"There's a picture of Barry Hines here," Crane points, crouching so his face is closer to a small black-and-white shot that shows a smattering of familiar faces.

"There's Bob Wilson, Dario Gradi, then Keith Blunt too. This is Ted Powell, who coached England's under-18s when Sol Campbell, the Nevilles and Nicky Butt came through, and Alan Bradshaw is here – that's probably doing a disservice not to mention the five other players in the picture too."

The wall of memories also includes other notable graduates, such as former Manchester United player Paul McGuinness, five-cap England goalkeeper Tony Waiters and the FA's long-serving Head of Player Development and Research, Andy Cale. But just as he pulls away from the treasure trove of names and stories in front of him, Crane spots someone else he knows very well.

"There's me," he exclaims with a little laugh. "And that is Rob (Matthews), who is just over there. He's got hair in this picture!"

OOOO

While Loughborough still holds a special place in the hearts of many alumni, not many come back for a second bite of the cherry. But that's exactly what Tom Curtis did.

Curtis had just finished a 400-match playing career that had taken in a host of Football League clubs, including Chesterfield and Portsmouth, when he returned to university for one final assignment.

With his playing days coming to an end, the midfielder wanted to get into coaching and saw an opportunity to join Loughborough's set-up as the perfect first step – just as it had been nearly 15 years earlier when he was a wet-behind-the-ears young pro.

While Curtis's stint as a geography and sports science student was punctuated by some stellar performances on the pitch, alongside a blossoming Football League career at Chesterfield, it was his second spell that left the biggest mark on Loughborough's history.

Teaming up with future Great Britain Universities Head Coach James Ellis, Curtis paved the way for the Scholars' return to non-league in 2007 and lay the groundwork for the club's transformation.

"James and I were keen on the university sides going into non-league and we were looking to get in the Midland Combination, as it was called back then," explains Curtis, who spent four years heading up the football programme, before leaving in 2011. "We wanted to give students a more rounded football experience. What we saw was the best players getting 16 games a season against a certain type of opposition in BUCS, then once they graduated, they'd go into non-league and not be used to that sort of playing style.

"The stadium was built as a direct result of us going into the non-league pyramid too. We wouldn't have got into the league if we hadn't committed to building a stadium and now it's a fantastic facility. For university football, it's got to be one of the best in the country by a long way."

Curtis's own experience as a student might have contributed to his belief that the university's footballers would benefit from more game time. He'd applied for a degree shortly after being released by Derby County as a young apprentice, but soon found himself with a place at Loughborough and a contract offer from nearby Chesterfield. Instead of choosing between the two, Curtis found a way to do both: as a full-time student and part-time player. With a foot in both camps, Curtis was able to benefit from three years in education – as well as turning out for Loughborough's BUCS side – while also gaining priceless experience in senior football.

"It ended up working pretty well because I played about 150 games for Chesterfield while I was studying," he says.

"It was quite unusual at the time and I don't think there were many other footballers doing it, but I just had to manage my time effectively and balance lectures with football and socialising. I never had nothing to do, but I've always liked being busy.

"My working week was training with the university side on Monday and Chesterfield on Tuesday, then playing in the BUCS game on

Wednesday. I'd train again for the university side on Thursday, then on Fridays I'd drive to Chesterfield straight from lectures to do set plays for the match on Saturday."

While looking at that sort of busy schedule might have left many students tearing their hair out, it proved to be worth the effort for Curtis.

By the time he'd graduated, he was a regular with Chesterfield in the third tier and was a key part of the side that went so close to reaching the 1997 FA Cup Final after losing to Middlesbrough in a semi-final replay.

It was the perfect grounding for a career in the game and was the springboard for Curtis to rack up hundreds of appearances over a 20-year playing career that ended, somewhat predictably, by pulling on the Loughborough purple while he was coaching there. And Curtis believes that if the university football programme can help any student follow in his footsteps and leave their mark on the game, it has been a success.

"Loughborough are a development team," he continues. "We never saw it as an end point for players; that's why we wanted to prepare players for non-league football. It should be an opportunity to help players get back into the pro game.

"There are all sorts of stories where we lost players to other clubs that could pay them money and we always saw that as a victory because we'd helped somebody make a living or earn a few bob from the game.

"University is an opportunity to get better at what you do and student sport is all about that too. There's lots of resource going into developing players in academy football, but people do get released if they haven't reached their full potential. Universities should be giving those late developers and people who have slipped through the net the chance to develop in a different environment."

It's no surprise that in the years since Curtis left Loughborough, development has been at the heart of everything he's done. And now he's one of a network of kingmakers who are hoping to help England's Three Lions roar to World Cup glory in the future.

As an FA youth coach developer, the 43-year-old is working with professional academies across the Midlands to cultivate the best young talent and give them the chance to blossom into fully fledged internationals who are capable of achieving success on the biggest stage.

It's a role that's not too dissimilar from his job at Loughborough. Curtis helps to identify top players who can have big futures in the game and works with their clubs so they can fulfil their potential. Only this time, the ultimate aim is to help the best performers win international caps rather than simply make a career.

"Development is something I've always been involved with and I enjoy it," Curtis says.

"I want to provide more opportunities for others and I enjoy this job because I'm helping people get better. The end goal is to provide outstanding players for the England national team, so we help the clubs and coaches. The aim of the whole directorate is to win the World Cup."

It's not the first time Curtis's eyes have been focused on the world's biggest prize. After reintroducing Loughborough into non-league and leading them to two BUCS league and cup doubles between 2008 and 2011, he swapped Leicestershire for the Caribbean to become Antigua and Barbuda's national team manager.

For the growing network of Loughborough alumni infiltrating the British game at every level, Curtis's venture to further climes stands out as one of the more unusual outposts. Curtis ranks as one of very few Loughborough alumni to ever get close to flying the university flag at a World Cup, with only Tony Waiters' achievement of leading Canada to the 1986 finals in Mexico standing as the sole example. But while Waiters managed the only team in Canada's history to compete at a World Cup, Curtis's task at Antigua and Barbuda was arguably even larger. A team lodged outside FIFA's top 100 before he arrived, the Benna Boys had ambitions of qualifying for their first World Cup. And with a nod to Loughborough's extra-curricular activities in the Midland Football League, Antigua and Barbuda entered their own club side into the UFL – the second tier of football in the US – to give their players more exposure to playing at a higher level. It meant that any illusions Curtis had of sipping a pina colada on an Antiguan beach while he waited for the next international break to roll round were soon shattered and instead, he and the team embarked on a road trip along the east coast for matches.

"There wasn't a lot of hanging out on the beach," Curtis laughs. "It was pretty flat out and for most of the summer, we were on the road. It was a good experience and very different. The job came about through a friend and I felt I needed a change, so I took the opportunity. It sounds like the football is a long way from over here, but we had some good players and were going up against the likes of the USA, Honduras and Panama in the CONCACAF qualifying zone."

While Curtis wasn't able to upset the odds and mastermind Antigua and Barbuda to World Cup qualification, he did achieve some notable landmarks: "We got into the last 12 of CONCACAF qualifying over the two years and reached the top 70 in the world, which was ahead of the likes of Wales and Northern Ireland at that particular time. It was an interesting experience," he adds.

○○○○

Kick-off is fast approaching in Loughborough and the alumni show no sign of relinquishing their prized area next to the glass windows that look out on to the pitch, perfectly nestled equidistant from full view of the match and the bar. If they're back on campus, why not enjoy the hospitality?

Outside, Loughborough's current crop of student footballers are readying themselves in the bitterly cold afternoon. A home match against Heanor Town would normally be a great chance for the Scholars to take all three points, but on current form, it looks like a daunting task. Heanor arrive comfortably in the top half of the table and with Loughborough's attention split across three fixtures per week, they are heading in the other direction. Their patchy form isn't helped by several first-teamers sitting in the stands injured and the untimely departures of two of their leading lights. Skipper Danny Brenan, who is in his final year, has jumped up two leagues to sign for Northern Premier League side Hednesford Town, while flying winger Jeremiah Dasaolu has moved to Grantham Town, where he'll earn a weekly wage.

Among the crowd of alumni, one man knows better than most what it's like to be coveted by clubs while studying at Loughborough. Only, no matter how hard some managers tried, Rob Matthews' answer was always no. Instead, the six-foot striker, who partnered Crane up front for the uni on many occasions, refused to consider the overtures he received from a series of Football League clubs until he donned his cap and gown to pick up his geography degree.

"I went for a trial at Manchester United before coming to Loughborough and looking back now, I don't think I took it seriously enough because I'd always wanted to go to university," he recalls, supping his pint as he watches the game.

"I didn't want to play professional football. I liked playing sport, particularly football, rugby and cricket, but it wasn't the be-all and end-all for me.

"Back in my first year, there was a Notts County scout who lived in Loughborough and he used to come and watch our games. By the end of my first year, I'd played a few games for their reserves and did the same in my second year.

"The manager at the time was Neil Warnock and I think he'd have signed me at the end of my second year, but I said no because I wanted to finish my degree. Perhaps I was a bit naïve, but even then I never really wanted to play pro football. I always envisaged getting a job after my degree, although when I got into my final year, I decided that football was probably the better option!"

After spurning the advances of a First Division team several times before, Matthews spent the Easter holiday between his final semesters training with Notts County. He borrowed a bike so he could get between Nottingham train station and the training ground, and was invited by Warnock to sit on the bench for a league match to get a feel for the big-match atmosphere. Although things didn't quite go to plan.

"Something happened the night before and somebody couldn't play," he reminisces, now reliving that moment 25 years earlier, rather than paying any attention to the pitch outside.

"Warnock obviously liked what I was doing. He told me I was on the bench, in the old First Division – now the Premier League – and I was just a student. I played 20 minutes and didn't do anything, but we won our first game in three months and it just went from there."

After playing under Warnock at Meadow Lane, Matthews went on to enjoy spells at several pro clubs, including Luton Town, Hull City and Bury, where he bumped into Warnock again.

Looking back at how it all began, Matthews puts a large part of his career down to his Loughborough experience – both on and off the pitch. It was at this campus that he grew up and it's where he cut his teeth as a footballer in BUCS competition and against professional reserve teams.

"If I'd gone into professional football as a teenager, I don't think it would have been for me," Matthews adds. "But coming to university and enjoying my time here, both socially and with the football, probably helped me. By 21, it was the right time for me, as a person, to go into football.

"Before I came here, I used to play lots of sports, but I concentrated on football once I got to Loughborough. We used to play university teams most Wednesdays, but also had 8 or 10 matches against reserve teams too, which got you out there. We played against Notts County, Aston Villa, Derby and Leicester, and I don't remember ever being beaten heavily – the mind boggles how they work it out to play so many matches nowadays.

"I stay in touch with more people from my time at Loughborough than the lads I played with professionally. When we catch up, we ask about the wife and kids, then we get on to talking about how it used to be."

Out on the pitch, the memories being created aren't so happy, particularly for Hafeez Sanusi. As a long ball over the top drops on the edge of the hosts' penalty area, the giant centre back is flattened by goalkeeper Conor O'Keefe who is rushing in the other direction. Both players fall flat on the ground, leaving Sanusi dazed, while the ball runs through for Jay Cooper to tap in. To make matters worse, Sanusi is withdrawn due to concussion.

Things get worse as the weakened backline allows Cooper to grab a second goal and while Alex Read pulls one back before the break, things aren't looking too good for Loughborough.

It hasn't put too much of a dampener on the alumni's day though, despite two carbon copy goals from corners at the beginning of the second half drawing a few groans from the group. The Scholars are 4-1 down and sinking without a trace.

Luke Trotman pulls one back to muted applause in the closing stages with a calm side-footed finish, but the alumni day will end in defeat.

"We won't let it spoil a good night," remarks one of the alumni, as the crowd disperses from outside and returns to the sanctity of the bar.

And they're not lying. An hour after the final whistle and with an almost empty room, the alumni are still here, working out whose round it is next, clinking their pint glasses as they go. It's like freshers' week all over again.

A RIGHT TO DREAM

There's less than half an hour until kick-off and Westfields still haven't arrived. The Hereford-based side are currently the toast of non-league after their giant-killing heroics brought them within minutes of reaching the FA Cup second round (five wins and three months further than the Scholars managed), but this isn't a case of the team letting their new-found fame go to their heads. Far from it. The team coach has been caught up in rush-hour traffic as they make one of the division's longest journeys – more than 100 miles – across the Midlands.

While Loughborough's squad fill one half of the floodlit pitch in preparation for kick-off, only a handful of Fields players populate the other. Kick-off has already been delayed and the crowd is awaiting news of the away side's arrival.

The mid-December chill that wraps around Loughborough University Stadium has forced many supporters back inside to keep warm. The camera set up to capture the match data and stream a live feed of a university match for the first time also lies in wait, patiently dormant, lens bowed until the action gets under way.

When the Westfields coach finally pulls through the barrier guarding the Holywell sports complex and parks up after its gruelling journey, the players hurriedly file off one-by-one. Among them is a guest who has more in common with his opponents than most of the Scholars team will realise.

That's because there's a student in Westfields' ranks. And he's more than familiar with juggling the commitments of education and semi-professional football. Although, despite the similarities now, his route to higher education has been different to any of Loughborough's students.

Sirdic Adjei Grant, or Sid to his teammates, cuts an unassuming figure. Possessing a slight frame in his Westfields tracksuit, Grant trots into the dressing room and heads out on to the pitch for a hasty warm-up. Tonight's match is the latest sub-chapter in a journey that the 20-year-old has taken from the Ghanaian capital of Accra. While many of his opponents are at university after collecting UCAS points through a variety of A levels, Grant has been totting up the air miles instead. And a Tuesday night game in wintry Loughborough is the next step in what he hopes is a journey that will take him to the Premier League and untold international honours.

On the face of it, Grant's dreams might seem like the naïve chunterings of an unreasonably ambitious youngster still plying his trade five divisions below the Football League but, in truth, it isn't so far-fetched.

OOOO

Grant is a student at Hartpury College, a further-education institute near Gloucester that has a reputation for helping young African footballers take the next step in their development. Linked with Right to Dream, an academy in West Africa that identifies talented children from across the continent to help them realise their potential, Hartpury offers youngsters the chance to sample English football while also getting an education. In the past, the college has provided a stepping stone for future international footballers, including Grant's fellow countrymen Majeed Waris and David Accam, who have both been capped several times for the Black Stars. And

Grant hopes he'll be next. But his path to stardom won't be a straightforward one. The midfielder is highly rated by many who watch him, but that reputation won't be enough for him to get a big move up the divisions any time soon. The FA won't allow it.

Grant knows that turning out in the Midland Football League is as good as it gets for him currently. That's because players on a student visa aren't allowed to play at a higher level than step five of the English football pyramid, so Grant is stuck beneath a glass ceiling he can't break through unless he moves to another country. But with a degree to study for, that's not a realistic option.

"I could probably play at around League One or League Two now if the visa wasn't an issue," Grant tells me when we caught up a couple of weeks before the Loughborough match.

"Although, whether I was a student or not, I would need to have made some appearances for my country to get a work permit and play at a higher level in England. When I have got my degree then, hopefully, I'll move elsewhere and get full-time football there."

This is Grant's second year playing in England. He spent last season pulling on the shirt of Westfields' cross-city neighbours Hereford, where he played a key role in the Bulls winning the Midland Premier Division title and reaching the FA Vase final at Wembley. But with the visa restrictions meaning Grant couldn't make the step up with his Hereford teammates, the match beneath Wembley's great arch was bittersweet for him. It was his last appearance for the Edgar Street side and it made losing 4-1 in the final to Northern League side Morpeth Town even harder to take.

Grant wasn't alone in that despair though. Winger Mustapha Bundu, from Sierra Leone, was also a gifted student from Hartpury College who saw his Hereford journey ended by promotion. Bundu, another of Right to Dream's bright young things, has since moved to Denmark to play for AGF Aarhus in the Danish Superliga, while Grant has found a new club to play for as he completes his degree. He didn't have to go far for his next move. Despite a host of interest from clubs in the region, the midfielder ended up moving just 350 yards from Hereford's Edgar Street ground to hole up at Westfields instead. Grant's next move is likely to be much further afield though.

"Bundu has gone to Denmark to play, which could also be an option for me when I finish at Hartpury," Grant says. "Hopefully, if things work out, Bundu will get the requirements he needs to come back here and play football. It was frustrating for both of us to not go any higher in England.

"I didn't think too much about promotion last season. I knew there was a possibility we'd do it, but I just focused on enjoying my football because I knew I couldn't go up with Hereford. At the end of the day, I couldn't do anything about it, so I just had to get my head down and keep playing.

"To play at England's national stadium was beautiful. A lot of professional players never get the chance to play there and I did with Hereford. It's a shame we didn't win, but it was still a dream come true."

Gracing Wembley's hallowed turf was an experience Grant's Hartpury predecessors Waris and Accam never achieved. The duo were at college at the same time and took their non-league apprenticeships at several clubs across the West Country, alongside competing in BUCS competitions as students. Since then, they have gone in different directions. Accam joined English manager Graham Potter (another with university links after taking his first coaching role at Leeds Metropolitan) at Swedish club Ostersunds, before moving on to Helsingborg and Chicago Fire in the MLS. Waris got his break at BK Hacken and earned a big move to Spartak Moscow, before settling in the French top flight at Lorient in 2015. Both of their journeys have been littered with international caps, with Waris even earning a place in Ghana's squad for the 2014 World Cup in Brazil. And it's success stories like those that inspired Grant to follow in their footsteps to Hartpury.

"The boys who are playing for the national team [Accam and Waris] both went to Hartpury, which was the main reason I went there too. Hopefully, I can do the same as them and find a team to sign me," adds Grant, who admits that his dream move is to play for Arsenal in the Premier League one day.

"Accam and Waris were three years above me at Right to Dream, so I know them. I contacted them both and asked them what it's like at Hartpury before making my final decision. They said it's fun and that the football here is good because you get to train in a full-time environment. Because people have come here in the same way and gone on to bigger things, I maintain a hope that I can get a degree, as well as help my football career."

Hartpury's football programme is different to Loughborough's. With no non-league side, they only offer between 10 and 13 competitive fixtures each season, which is why the better players must look elsewhere for extra game time. But it's not a case of players fending for themselves, as there are strong links between the college and several clubs in the area, including Football League sides Swindon Town, Bristol City and Exeter City.

The quality of Hartpury's football programme is reflected in their dominance of the BUCS Premier Division South (the league running parallel to Loughborough's), having won eight of the past nine titles and taking four national championships in the past decade. This year is no different, with Hartpury vying for top spot again.

For Grant, success on the football pitch isn't all he wants to measure his time at Hartpury by. While Right to Dream has helped to give African children a route to a new life on the football pitch, giving talented youngsters an education is equally, if not more, important.

Born to two working parents in Ghana, Grant has already seen a new side to the world that they have never sampled. Before enrolling at Hartpury, he represented Right to Dream at tournaments across Europe, so is used to being away from home. In the five years after being snapped up by Right to Dream, Grant's passport was stamped plenty of times. He went to France, Germany and Spain, before travelling to Abu Dhabi with Manchester City's academy, thanks to another Right to Dream association. He could even have taken a qualification in the US, if Hartpury's pull hadn't turned his head towards leafy Gloucestershire. Grant's parents have always been supportive of his career and they encouraged him to make the sacrifices he needed to, such as staying at his former manager's house to make sure he got to training and matches while playing in Accra. So after seeing what a life in professional football promises, it's no surprise that Grant wants to be involved in the game no matter what.

"I want to have a solid foundation and back-up plan I can rely on if playing doesn't work out. That's why studying at Hartpury is so important," he continues.

"I'd want to stay in the sport even if I don't make it as a player, probably something like a technical director or a coach. I have done my FA Level One coaching badge at Hartpury, so maybe I could do more of those qualifications too.

"By travelling around with Right to Dream, I have seen that football is a better life and it's opened my eyes to another world. It's not about the money of being a top player – you can make money in different ways – if I make it big, I'll be doing it for the football."

○○○○

Out on Loughborough's pitch, Grant and his Westfields teammates are having a rare off day. Loughborough, who have been out of sorts in the league of late, are back at close to full strength and are matching their opponents all over the park.

Chasing, harrying and pressing, the students are full of energy, maybe buoyed by an end-of-term buzz before they go away on a well-earned Christmas break.

Grant is the antithesis of the Scholars' zest. The wide midfielder looks jaded and struggles to call upon the boundless effect he usually injects into games. While Loughborough are able to rotate their large performance squad to keep players as fresh as possible, Westfields' FA Cup heroes are part of a small core that is coping with a demanding fixture list, lengthened by success in the knock-out competition.

That said, they're still formidable opponents. They're many people's favourites to follow in neighbours Hereford's footsteps and gain promotion out of the league, and sit within 11 points of leaders Alvechurch, with six games in hand.

Westfields are big and solid, and pose a threat at set pieces, which have been an Achilles' heel for Loughborough all season, especially since towering defender Danny Brenan left last month. But the Scholars look assured and despite a couple of nervy moments, they repel the visitors whenever they come forward.

Grant is withdrawn shortly before the hour-mark. For all the expectation, he has struggled and leaves the pitch to little ceremony. It's in stark contrast to his appearance at Loughborough last season, when he rampaged down the right flank in perfect harmony with his Hereford teammates as they trounced the Scholars 5-0. It's a performance that highlights how far Grant still has to come. As a 20-year-old with a busy schedule to contend with, inconsistency can be expected, but it's not how the Ghanaian will have wanted to perform against his fellow students.

Not long after Grant has settled down on the bench, matters get worse for Westfields. Loughborough winger Alex Read shows his quality to cut inside and put Loughborough ahead with a powerful effort. But just as it looks as though the hosts are set to claim an unexpected scalp, an old weakness rears its ugly head. As the large scoreboard ticks towards the final whistle, a deep cross from the right wing isn't cut out at the back post and the ball drops for Westfields substitute Richard Greaves, who is given enough time to convert from a few yards out.

The students are gutted as the visiting bench goes wild. It's a bitter pill to swallow and the late equaliser means they'll have to settle for a point. It was a display similar to the encouraging performances that delighted at the beginning of the season and offers new hope that results will change.

For Grant, he'll be covering more miles. As he jumps in the car to head back towards Gloucestershire, that familiar sensation of travelling takes over again. He might not have shone brightly tonight, but there's a feeling that wherever the Ghanaian's final destination is, he'll have one hell of an experience getting there.

ALL ROADS LEAD
TO ROCESTER

It's Boxing Day morning and I'm rummaging about in the cupboard under my stairs. I've been in there for a couple of minutes, looking in bags and lifting boxes that have lay dormant for months. But I still can't find my treasure. I know it's in there. Somewhere. Then I set eyes on it. Peeking out of a small blue-and-black bag, alongside an old tennis racket and a couple of well-hidden linesman flags.

I've found my football boots – and they might just come in useful for this afternoon's trip to watch Loughborough's match against Rocester. That's right, while most people are enjoying yet another dive into the festive buffet and slobbing out with the family in front of Indiana Jones for the umpteenth time, I'm clinging on to the distant, if a little naïve, hope that I might make my senior football debut. What if, under some quirk of circumstance, I need my boots. I couldn't leave them at home, just in case. The fantasy that awoke in my mind a week or so earlier would always haunt me if I missed my chance because I'd left my boots at home.

The thought of getting out on the pitch first hit me when I was chatting to Skubala at half-time during the match against Westfields earlier in the month. I brought up the topic of Christmas, which I've learned is a bit of a taboo subject at Loughborough. With all the students going home between terms, numbers are notoriously thin on the ground and it's no different this year. Skubala had told me earlier in the season that there is no expectation for any of the players to make it back for the festive fixtures. After all, for some who live halfway across the country and don't own a car, there is no discernible way for them to reach matches: especially a Boxing Day contest to be played in a tiny Staffordshire village. So after Skubala gave me a wry smile that preluded an admission that it looked as though only nine of the students could make it to Rocester for the game, the cogs in my brain had started winding at the prospect of getting out on the pitch myself.

"Can you play?" Skubala asked me when I first raised the idea of me adding to Loughborough's dwindling numbers for today's match.

"Err… I still play a bit of five-a-side now and then," I said, hoping that my cover hadn't been blown before I could start telling him about the time that, as a 13-year-old, I'd been to a training session run by then-Sunderland manager Peter Reid after my junior team won a competition.

"I mean at this level. Can you play in non-league?" he asked again. I could already feel his interest waning.

I'd gone on to give him a non-committal answer that neither confirmed or denied if I was up to the task, and we talked about FA player registration (OK, I mentioned registration). But as I went to find my seat for the second half, I still clung on to the idea that I might sneak on to the bench. And that's why I find myself sorting through clutter to put together an emergency playing kit to leave in the back of my car in case I'm needed when I reach the ground.

As I drive along the tight country roads that line the final 10 miles of my journey to Rocester, it soon becomes clear just how unkind the fixture list has been to Loughborough. Even as my satnav informs me that I'm getting closer to the end destination, I still haven't seen many signs that confirm I'm heading in the right direction. How can you expect any non-drivers to make it here?

I'm driving past farms, local shopping outposts and a seemingly endless sheet of fields that boast a menagerie of animals in them, but can't see anything that suggests I'm close to any sort of settlement, let alone one that is capable of hosting a football match.

Just as I'm about to pull over and check that I've typed the correct address into the satnav, I finally spot a sign to Rocester. The next left takes me on to an even tighter road, where I pass a pheasant, carelessly bobbing about dangerously close to the camber. This couldn't be any further from the Premier League juggernaut that English football is known for.

Rocester is one of those places that could easily be missed if you blinked. Home to just 1,700 people, the village sits in a small area between the River Churnet and the River Dove, and contains a small collection of houses with a single church at its centre. There's no train station and, as I'm finding, limited road links to the surrounding world.

After picking my way through the country lanes, I finally see Rocester's Hillsfield ground. Through the sparse trees that provide a buffer between the terrace that stands in line with the road outside, I can see the two teams beginning their warm-ups.

The cold wind I can feel hitting my car as I turn past the imposing JCB Academy, which is housed in an 18th-century mill, opposite the ground's entrance, brings with it another icy blast: disappointment. From what I can see, there are enough Loughborough players to make up a full squad for the match. Perhaps my hope of earning a place on the subs' bench was nothing more than a pipedream.

After entering the single turnstile at the corner of the ground closest to the old mill, I make a beeline for the teamsheet to see how makeshift

Loughborough's team is for today's match. The nine students that Skubala had told me about are in the side and are joined by two external players, Alex Johnson and Lee Miveld, who are local players regularly called upon to offer much-needed experience to the young side throughout the season. The bench is made up of more familiar names, with messrs Skubala, Brennan and Mat providing cover, alongside 17-year-old Loughborough Dynamo loanee Dan Tuck.

The squad is threadbare, and with Skubala and Brennan putting the players through their paces rather than warming up themselves, it's clear that they don't expect to be rolling back the years, unless injuries leave them with no other alternative.

"I'm a bit nervous about this, so I was glad when I saw we'd got everyone here," admits Mat, after practising goal kicks with regular glovesman James Stallan.

"I've played at this level in my local league when I was younger, but I haven't done it properly for about four years. I'd worried that James wasn't going to get here and I'd have to start in goal – and I'm not sure I'm prepared for that!"

This isn't the first time that Mat and the other back-room staff have been called upon to make up the numbers. In fact, Mat found himself in between the sticks last season when Conor O'Keefe was sent off against Heanor Town. He kept a clean sheet that day.

Mat, Skubala and Brennan, along with assistant Ricky Nurse, were also named on the bench together last Christmas but so far, other than Mat's sole appearance, they haven't made it on to the pitch yet.

In the time since the Scholars have been back in non-league, they have thrown together a team of elder statesman on one previous occasion. With student players at an even greater premium, Loughborough cobbled together a team made up of alumni to play in a league match. Despite their opponents' initial confusion at what appeared to be the oldest collection of university students there'd ever been, it proved to be a master stroke, with the new-look (or old-look, depending which way you look at it) team running out victorious.

There was no need to go to such limits today, largely due to the dedication of some of the players to get to Rocester. Not only did the players have to resist the temptation to get a second helping of pigs in blankets yesterday, many of them were up early this morning and heading out on the road to get to the game in plenty of time for kick-off too.

Captain-for-the-day Drew Bridge has travelled from Salisbury to be here, while goalkeeper Stallan left early to arrive from Guildford in Surrey. There are similar stories across the entire side, with the shortest journey of any of the students being Tom Rankin's 50-mile trek from the outskirts of Birmingham.

The cold, blustery conditions are enough to blow away any of the post-Christmas cobwebs that still remain, although not everything is going smoothly. With only minutes before kick-off, Miveld grabs Brennan in the centre of the pitch. He's pulled up with a calf strain in the warm-up and won't be able to start the match. The Scholars, already down to the bare bones, will have to throw in 17-year-old Tuck for his debut, leaving only the team who normally man the dugout as backup if anybody else goes down injured. If that wasn't enough of a concern, Bridge and Tom Barnes, who are both more recognised forwards, are now being deployed as auxiliary full backs on either flank.

As I settle down in a small fold-away wooden chair in the tiny main stand, I try to shield myself from the low sun and chilly winds that are gusting across the pitch. The reality is, I'm sitting a lot more comfortably than anybody on the Loughborough bench.

Things start to look a little better within a minute. Barnes pings a pass into Johnson's feet and the midfielder turns swiftly to play in Alex Read. The winger is engulfed by yellow shirts, so he plays the ball quickly into the path of Rankin, who arrows a low 20-yard effort into the bottom corner of the net. What was everyone worried about?

It's a start that's caught more than just Rocester's players off guard. The scattering of home supporters grows over the next few minutes, with one fan telling the late arrivals that the team must have eaten too much Christmas pudding. As the stand fills up, a grey-haired man is unceremoniously dragged into his seat by two border collies, who show their support by barking in unison when the ball comes anywhere near the Loughborough goal.

Thankfully, there isn't much sign of that happening and the away side's good start almost gets even better. Rankin finds himself in the clear again and goes within inches of slotting a second beyond Richard Froggatt in the hosts' goal, but a late stretch sees the goalkeeper parry it away to safety.

Just past the half-hour mark, the visitors go even closer to doubling their advantage. Barnes, who appears to be revelling in his new full back role, crosses into Ben Ward-Cochrane, the ball sitting up nicely for the striker as he unleashes a half-volley that flies past Froggatt and comes back off the inside of the post.

Rocester aren't called the Romans for nothing though (in reality, it's because Hillsfield is positioned in the middle of a former Roman fort) and they're determined to go down fighting.

A long pass is hoicked up towards Loughborough's backline and catches in the wind, leaving Joe Jackson flat-footed. Oliver Roome charges towards the pass, getting away from Jackson, only for the defender to swing round his man and clear the ball, taking Roome with him.

The whistle blows and the collies go mad while the home support cry blue murder. The referee races across and points towards an area outside of the box, signalling a free kick rather than the penalty most people expect. Then, he delves into his pocket to produce the one Christmas card the Scholars didn't want to see: a red for Jackson. The defender can hardly believe it and puts his hands to his head before trudging off towards the tunnel.

The resulting free kick comes to nothing, but it's the least of Loughborough's worries. With a patched-up defence already, they are forced to drop Rankin back to plug the gap in the middle. There are no real options on the bench to change things tactically and now the 10 remaining players are facing more than 50 minutes with a man down.

Jackson's dismissal changes the entire complexion of the match. Loughborough were in control and looking to be well on their way to victory, but that's clearly changed as the teams return for the second half. Almost immediately after the restart and Rocester have the ball in the net. Jackson's nemesis Roome gets on the end of a back-post corner, but the celebrations are turned to confusion as the referee rules out the goal. Somehow, the Scholars survive.

That good fortune soon runs out. Romans right back James Frost kicks a high, spinning ball into the area, which deceives almost everybody, before dropping to Martyn Smythe, who makes the most of the space to take a touch and belt a powerful effort through Stallan to equalise.

Surely, an under-strength Loughborough side with less men are going to succumb to Rocester now. Apparently not.

While Skubala and Brennan remain unmoved on the touchline,

showing no sign of replacing any of the players, the 10 men get a second wind. Not only do they manage to repel the Romans as they come forward, but Alex Dinsmore almost puts them ahead with a low effort that's saved. Then with the clock ticking away, Read embarks on a mazy run from the halfway line. He slaloms one way, then the next to find space in the box and leaves defenders in his wake. But just as he's about to pull the trigger, a fallen defender appears to handle the ball on the ground. The referee remains unmoved and Read jinks again to get a shot off that bounces back off the underside of the crossbar. Ward-Cochrane gets to the rebound and after seeing his first follow-up blocked, his second shot is held by Froggatt. It's not to be, the match finishes 1-1.

Loughborough's heroic efforts can't truly be appreciated until after the match, as the players tell their stories of sacrifices and long-distance jaunts to get out on the pitch. There are family gatherings missed, 350-mile-round trips and unseasonal restraint at the Christmas dinner table, but it's all been worth it.

"Once you get over the initial effort of having to come up here and get out on the pitch, you almost put even more effort in," says Bridge as he walks to his car ready for the three-and-a-half-hour journey back to Salisbury.

"Everyone has come from all over to be here, so you pull together for the team – there was a really good feel out there today and there was no getting beaten. In the past two seasons, we've struggled at Christmas and come away with no points from four or five games, so things are already going better this year."

Despite his best attempts, Bridge's hopes of bringing a bit of Christmas cheer with him on the long drive were thwarted. Well, apart from a single turkey sandwich, that is.

"All of the family are round today, so it's likely to be pretty hectic back home. My dad was desperate to come with me, but mum was having none of it and wouldn't let him leave," he adds with a grin.

"There were hams, cheese, crackers – everything at home, but I wasn't allowed to touch anything. All I was allowed to leave with was a turkey sandwich with cranberry sauce on it so, hopefully, there'll be some leftovers when I get back."

As Bridge sets off for home, his tale would be the most forlorn of the day if it wasn't for the fact that my football boots are sitting unused in my car.

D-DAY RECKONING

It's a Wednesday afternoon ritual that has been repeated for decades. Hosts of students wearing purple and black Loughborough hoodies trickle into campus carrying training bags, boots and an assortment of other sporting equipment. Wednesday is the day that studies take a back seat for a few hours. Where sporting competition is the be-all and end-all.

This week is no different than any other. In fact, in some ways it matters even more than usual. That's because it's D-day: the one time a year when Loughborough play host to their biggest rivals, Durham University. The top-ranked sport university in the country against the second. The undisputed champions for the past 35 years and the great pretenders.

Across the entire campus, Loughborough's best sports teams are preparing to face their adversaries from the north-east in a series of athletic duels. With the first kick-offs of the day fast approaching, students are lining the pathways and heading towards where they'll be watching – or playing for – the home team.

Loughborough's campus looks unlike almost any other in Britain. Along with the tall buildings packed with lecture theatres and the student accommodation dotted around, a number of impressive stadiums stick out. It's almost like a miniature Olympic Park. There are hockey, athletics and cricket grounds, with arching stands that sprout out of the terrain, and a large rugby pitch that sits in the centre of the campus.

As D-day slowly awakens from its slumber, a buzz of anticipation is beginning to build. One of the day's first fixtures is taking place on the outskirts of the peppy sports community, as Loughborough's football team go up against Durham. But the match won't be held in the impressive football stadium as initially planned. The game has been moved to the Nike Academy pitch, which is one of the three fields that sit alongside it.

"The stadium pitch took a battering on Saturday and there's been a lot of rain since, so the groundsman has asked us to move it," Mat tells me as I arrive. "It's a shame because it'd be good to have a big match in the stadium, but there's not a lot we can do."

While the stadium is the football team's home, they're at the behest of the university, as its owners. So if the pitch is declared unplayable by the groundsman, the decision is taken out of the club's hands.

Thankfully, as it's a BUCS fixture, the match can still take place on one of the outside pitches. That means a long walk between dressing rooms and pitchside: over the adjoining bridge, past a sodden beach volleyball court and up a hill. There'll be no nervous wait in the tunnel before today's grudge match.

For what the occasion loses by the late change in location, it is more than made up for by what's at stake. It's not all about university pride, with Loughborough and Durham only separated by a single point at the top of BUCS Premier North. With D-day coinciding with the final day of the league season, the rivalry will decide who finishes top – the stakes couldn't be much higher.

The Scholars currently hold the advantage, with a one-point lead at the top of the table, so Durham will have to win to take first place. That'll be no mean feat on current form. After a stuttering start that saw Loughborough languishing at the bottom of the six-team division, they won the next five games to reach the summit.

While there has been a nearly two-month gap between the last BUCS fixtures because of the Christmas holiday, Loughborough have improved in the Midland Football League too: collecting nine points through late-December and New Year to ease any concerns that they might get dragged into a relegation battle.

Although it's the only prize anyone is focused on today, topping the league isn't the biggest achievement in BUCS football. That will be competed for in the weeks after this match, with the national championship pitting the best teams from all over the country against each other in a straight knock-out tournament. Both Loughborough and Durham have already qualified for the end-of-season competition, although whoever wins the league will receive a bye into the last 16 and be guaranteed a home tie in the quarter-final. Victory could make all the difference.

After a wet few days in Leicestershire, Team Durham will be delighted that their trip from the north-east hasn't been for nothing. The rain that looked set in a couple of hours ago has abated and the pitch appears to be holding up well as the two teams begin their warm-ups.

In some ways, the game being brought outside of the stadium is a benefit to the visitors. Loughborough's facilities are the envy of most other universities in the division, so to take on the players out on a pitch without large stands and daunting high buildings surrounding it might be an advantage. Although it would be doing the Nike pitch a disservice to say it is undistinguished. The pitch is in the second of three football fields that form a row next to the stadium. But with a climb up a steep hill to reach the touchline, it gives the impression of being elevated above everything else and provides a great vantage point for the rest of the university, as it sprawls out into the distance.

The ground was once the home of the Nike Academy, who used to train and play matches at the university before moving to the FA's St. George's Park headquarters a couple of years ago. The pitch has maintained its eponymous name and still sports the black-and-white hoardings emblazoned with Nike artwork around the edge of the field.

As the game isn't a non-league fixture and the match day volunteers aren't around to offer a helping hand, luxuries such as a teamsheet are at a premium and most of the gathering supporters are left to pick out who they know for themselves. Even before I catch a glimpse of the referee's official form with the starting line-ups on, which is being passed between the dugouts, one player stands out as the teams go through their final preparations. It's the captain Danny Brenan and he's taking pride of place in the back four, who are practising defensive clearances.

Heading a couple of hanging passes away in unison with his fellow defenders, Brenan has been missed since he moved up a couple of divisions to play for Hednesford Town. He still retains dual registration, which allowed him to play for the Scholars in a Midland Premier League match last month when the Pitmen weren't in action, so the transfer hasn't stopped him keeping his place in the BUCS team. It's all part of the support and development that Loughborough's management team promise to their performance squad. Players can move on, but they can still call in on Skubala and co for advice and stay involved in the full-time programme alongside their new club's schedule, if they want to. In that way, university football really is like nothing else.

Within minutes of kick-off, Brenan is showing just what Loughborough have been missing for the past two months. The centre back, resplendent in his captain's armband, looks a cut above as he marshalls his troops to battle: batting away Durham attacks and barking orders to his teammates.

It's a different sort of contest to the ones I've seen Brenan play in previously. In non-league, teams are more direct and wily strikers provide different challenges on every outing, whereas Durham are more subtle in their approach.

Brenan clearly wants to show what his time at Hednesford has already taught him and is taking more responsibility for his duties as a senior player, jostling opponents as he steps out from the back to win duels and bellowing instructions at any given time. Even Durham's players aren't immune to Brenan's words – or his tackles.

After a heavy touch nestles midway between the big defender and Durham number eight Philpott, Brenan launches off the ground to take the ball but takes a large portion of the man too. Philpott's teammates scream blue murder and call for the referee to take action, a shout that Brenan bats off with a smirk and a burst of colourful language. He must have learned that at Hednesford.

While Brenan is fortunate to escape with just a telling off, it's Durham who are counting their lucky stars moments later. Speedy winger Christian Enerenadu skips in from the left and lays on a pass for Alex Dinsmore, but he steers his effort narrowly wide of the post.

By now, scores of people have joined the edge of the pitch to cheer on the home team. A normal BUCS game usually draws nothing worthy of calling a crowd, but today's showdown has clearly piqued the interest of many. The numbers have been boosted by parents and prospective students, invited along for an experience day to get a taste of Loughborough's football programme and there are many other current students who have made the trip too.

Before kick-off, Skubala had warned the players not to go out to play for the draw they needed to clinch top spot and they appear to have taken notice. They look comfortable and enjoy most of the possession but are lacking the final pass or touch to take full advantage. And the Scholars are nearly made to pay. Goalkeeper James Stallan spills a free kick from the left, then regathers before one of Durham's forwards pounces, leaving him to smother a poorly judged back pass, with Wykes lurking.

The away side are buoyed by Loughborough's fallibilities and create a fantastic opening when Cornish delivers a fizzing cross across the face of goal and Philpott slides within inches of giving Durham the lead.

I'm starting to feel nervous and I'm not the only one. First-team coach Alex Ackerley, a former student who joins Skubala in the dugout for BUCS matches, paces up and down the touchline, scrunching up a piece of paper as the Scholars live increasingly dangerously. His anxiety only heightens as a couple of promising Loughborough attacks break down due to careless touches.

Enerenadu is Loughborough's best outlet. He manoeuvres inside from the left again, twisting, tying his full back in knots. He makes a couple of yards of space to square to Ben Last. Ackerley sucks in a sharp intake of breath, then pirouettes in frustration as Last's strike is parried away.

The ever-impressive Luke Trotman is next to try and unpick the defensive lock. The former Luton man jinks between two men on the edge of the penalty area and as he looks up to pick out a man, he's sent tumbling to the ground. The whistle goes and both sides appeal to the referee, who wants to confirm his suspicions with his assistant on the near side.

There's a nervous few seconds as everybody focuses their attention on the officials' conversation. Is it a penalty, a free kick or even a dive? Then, the referee turns and points to the spot. Penalty to Loughborough.

Jack Poxon steps up to take the kick and converts just out of the Durham keeper's reach. It's 1-0 and right on half-time. Nearly there.

Now is the time to test the mettle of Loughborough's class of 2017. A goal behind, Durham must be less conservative in an attempt to find the two strikes they need to steal the crown in the Scholars' backyard.

It's easier said than done, as they struggle to penetrate Brenan's superbly organised backline, which leaves long-range efforts as the most direct route to Loughborough's goal. That's exactly the route substitute McGrath takes as he angles a drive at goal that causes Stallan to fly to his right to turn it away.

The hosts continue to soak up the pressure and hit back on the break. Poxon takes a potshot from 30 yards out, only to see it nick the post on the way wide as he tries to double his side's slender advantage.

While it stays at one goal, everyone is on tenterhooks, especially the animated Ackerley, whose constant pacing along the technical area is the polar opposite of Skubala's calm demeanour.

OOOO

Some people just seem destined for the dugout. Whether it's what they say or do, their studious nature or innovative way of thinking, there's a tell-tale sign. For Alex Ackerley, it was something he didn't do.

Growing up in the idyllic Yorkshire Dales, among miles of rolling hills populated by sheep and cows, Ackerley was always a football nut. Despite the beautiful green expanse around him, his draw was always to those patches of outdoor space that had been transformed into football pitches, with a series of drawn-out white lines and two goalposts.

When he wasn't playing football, he was watching it. When he wasn't watching football, he was thinking about it. But despite his fascination for the game, there was never just one club that garnered his infatuation. He never had a team to call his own. Not truly.

"I've abstained from being a football fan, as boring as that sounds," he unloads, as though revealing a deep, hidden secret.

"I used to have a Manchester United season ticket at Old Trafford with my dad, but it got to the point where I was playing in a game on the Saturday and then two more on a Sunday, so I gave up going.

"Within football coaching in England, there is too much subjectivity and emotional overflow, so I've had to retract that part of my mind because you become too subjective and emotionally amped by the sport. It's too easy to get carried away, however boring that is."

Even without his admission that he purposefully avoids the pitfalls of football fandom, anyone spending just a few minutes in Ackerley's company will be instantly struck by his maturity. At just 24-years-old, the coach might look fresh-faced when he's pacing around in the technical area on a match day, but his attitude is that of somebody much older. He talks with authority, an ability that helps enormously with coaching, and has endless reams of football knowledge that means he holds his own in any conversation, no matter who he's speaking to.

It was some of those qualities that must have leaped out to Skubala when he gave Ackerley, a graduate from the previous year, the chance to stay on with the first team to develop his talents alongside him on the university's quest for BUCS success.

Ackerley is a coaching veteran by the university's standards, having been closely involved with several football teams at Loughborough since he enrolled on a sports and exercise science degree at the age of 18 – supplementing that with a post-graduate sports coaching qualification.

"I started coaching at 19 for the women's club, then did the men's threes last year," Ackerley recounts.

"Through coaching the third team last year and doing what I hope was a good job, Skubes [Skubala] knew I was staying in Loughborough and asked if I wanted to step up to help on the BUCS team on Wednesdays, which I grabbed with two hands. It's a good level to work at for somebody of my age and experience.

"I've also started coaching at Burton Albion academy this year, which is something separate to the university. I applied for a part-time role there and got it, along with another of the coaches here. While it wasn't linked to the university, it did help being local and having the experience."

As a hotbed for young sportsmen, Loughborough's reputation for providing chances for prospective coaches is strong. With so many teams playing at a high standard, there is ample opportunity for students with the suitable drive and ability to have a crack at realising their dreams. Ackerley is a prime example of how that approach can bear fruit.

"I've climbed through the ranks of the student football club," he says in the booming tones that accompany many a Yorkshireman's accent. "Each team has at least two coaches and there are six teams, so that's 12 coaches straightaway. Those positions are open, and then there's the analysts and sports scientists as well, so there's lots of opportunity to get involved.

"I've come on a huge amount since I started – the difference can't be quantified as such. The main thing is the experience and from the first year through to six years in, working with so many different players and coaches has been the most beneficial thing. You pick up many different things from every coach you work with: what's good practice and what isn't. You try to put that together into one."

With money set aside for the student coaches to subsidise any coaching badges throughout the year as well, it's clearly another breeding ground for people who need to get their foot on the first rung of the football ladder.

Although Ackerley didn't arrive at Loughborough with coaching as his main goal, his passion for football soon transferred on to the training pitch. Using a mixture of the values he's seen from his parents, who both work in training and development roles outside of sport, and absorbing the unique experience he is sampling at Loughborough, the young coach has his eyes set firmly on a long coaching career.

His long-term aim is to start coaching in the older age groups at professional academies and establish himself as a permanent member of staff at a club. Although Ackerley realises it'll take more than a few BUCS games to do that, so is just focused on soaking up every ounce of his current environment that he can.

"Coaching at Loughborough has been quite an educational experience," he ponders. "As soon as you're in the first team, you've got to deal with the whole programme side of it: games on Tuesday nights, Wednesdays, Saturdays, so there are a lot more factors to deal with other than just turning up to coach.

"When you're managing such a big squad of 30 people, it is a challenge to get everyone flying in the same direction, so when changes need to be made, it can disrupt the flow a bit. We also do an alright job of keeping them on task when it comes to dealing with other parts of student life that can sometimes turn people's heads.

"Higher-education football is a good place to work. It's development and performance, and you can send people off to so many places – whether it's higher up or in the pro game, or doing a masters in the US."

○○○○

"Come on lads, give me a little bit more," shouts Ackerley, as the ball goes out for a throw-in on the far side. "Show me more."

Geeing up the team on the sideline, Ackerley anxiously stops and rests his hand on his chin, as he watches the next phase of play develop. Durham have the ball as they attempt to pierce a way through. One pass to the next, then across to the other side: constantly picking and probing for a gap to thrust in a decisive attack.

Then one of the passes is misplaced inside Durham's half and presents Read with a chance to get away. The winger makes up ground and tees up Poxon on the edge of the area, providing just enough room for the former Oldham trainee to rattle a right-footed strike into the net. Coming towards the end of his final year studying at Loughborough, Poxon could be on the verge of giving the university something to really remember him by.

While the goal settles the nerves a bit, Durham still pour forward to try and find the three goals they need to win. And they start getting closer to making the breakthrough: King drawing a save from Stallan and Philpott dragging an effort wide from inside the area.

With the game running into its final minutes, Loughborough's defence is breached. And, not surprisingly, it's from a set piece. Even Brenan's presence in the box can't stop a deep free kick finding its way to the unmarked Paull to force home at the back post.

The unlikely comeback might be on, but when Cornish fires wide from close range and Stallan rises to confidently punch away another set piece, the victory is confirmed. Loughborough have won the league.

However, if they're going to win the national championship to become this year's top university football team, Loughborough's latest vintage will have to overcome several more universities with unique approaches of their own.

LEADING THE WAY

It's not just at Loughborough where university football is taking a novel approach. More than 300 miles north and beyond Hadrian's Wall, Stirling University in Scotland is breaking through social barriers all of their own.

When Shelley Kerr was hired as the university's high-performance men's coach in 2014, she became the UK's first female football manager to take charge of a male team and nearly three years on, she remains the country's one and only. The 59-cap former Scotland international is a highly respected figure in the women's game, having picked up three trophies in just 16 months as manager of Arsenal Ladies, but it was still a surprise to many when she was given the nod to take over Stirling's men's team. In fact, it even seemed to surprise Kerr.

"I'd applied to do a masters in sports management at Stirling and the job subsequently became available, so I applied in the hope that I would have the opportunity of getting an interview at least," she tells me when I meet her before a league match in February.

"Thankfully, it worked out for me and I got the job. It was the perfect fit for me and the university. I'm a great believer that you need to start somewhere, gain experience and do it the right way. And the university was forward-thinking in appointing me. Would a football club have made the appointment at that point? Probably not. Would they now? I don't know: only owners and chief execs at clubs will know the answer to that."

Sadly, it seems that the world of football is still several years behind the education sector. Only former England women's boss Hope Powell has ever even been spoken about in the same breath as a managerial vacancy at a British men's club, when she was rumoured to be in discussions about taking the Grimsby Town role in 2009. That talk was swiftly denied by Powell.

However, when Kerr's application came up in front of Stirling University's panel, her CV and enthusiasm for the post stood out above everybody else's – and her gender wasn't given a second thought as she was offered the post.

Despite being an unprecedented appointment for British football, it's a move that has paid off for both Stirling and Kerr. The university's first team compete alongside Loughborough in BUCS Premier North and just like their fellow students, play in senior football as part of the Lowland Football League, Scotland's fifth tier. And with second- and third-place finishes in the respective divisions last season, the results on the pitch are going well.

With a packed fixture list to contend with already, Kerr's remit also includes looking after Stirling University's under-20s team, which offers first-year scholars the chance to play regular football, meaning the 47-year-old spends most of her time either on the training pitch or in the dugout.

Kerr's work ethic is just one of many reasons why she is so cherished north of the border. With a stack of coaching qualifications and more top-level experience than most managers in this realm of Scottish football, her legend has been growing among her peers for years.

While many Scottish coaches – including today's opposition manager, East Kilbride boss Martin Lauchlan – see her as a glowing example of what can be achieved against more traditional barriers, Kerr is only focused on the job in hand. She won't be taken in by the moniker she carries due to her gender and as the media spotlight initially shone in her direction when she was appointed in 2014, Kerr was more interested in getting to grips with managing players with contrasting priorities. University football, after all, is a player development path like no other.

"There is a huge shift in the mindset of the players between when they first enter the programme and when they finish," she explains, after I ask her what has stood out to her during the transition from Women's Super League to university football.

"At first, the players still have dreams of becoming professional footballers, but by the last season, they're very focused on getting a degree. It sets them up because, as we all know, unless you're playing at the highest level, it can be difficult to make a living out of football, especially in Scotland. If the players can get a degree and get back into the pro game, that is brilliant and that's what the programme is designed to do."

Kerr is leading her charges from the touchline in a Lowland League match against league leaders East Kilbride. While Stirling University have been playing some of their home games in this division at the 7,937-capacity Falkirk Stadium, today's surroundings are noticeably smaller.

At just a tenth of the attendance in Falkirk, East Kilbride's K-Park Training Academy has a different feel to it. A solitary seated stand is all that protects me from the cold Scottish winds that are gusting across the artificial pitch that the two teams will do battle on. The ground is smart but compact. At a capacity of just 660, the stadium is in the heart of a community sports complex in Calderglen Park, which includes the home grounds of the town's rugby and cricket teams, as well as tennis courts, a golf course and a mini zoo. It's a world away from the sort of grounds Kerr visited in her most recent job as gaffer at Arsenal Ladies.

Although it wasn't just the difference in the facilities that Kerr had to familiarise herself with after taking up the role in Stirling; it was managing a university team that took some getting used to as well.

"The academic side was a different environment for me at first because I needed to have a bit of sympathy for what the players were going through as part of their academic cycle," Kerr explains.

"It's difficult for me as a coach because I want to win games, but I also have to see the bigger picture. There is nothing more rewarding than seeing someone graduate with a degree at the end of their four years and potentially go back into the professional game, so I need to give them a good balance from both perspectives.

"That was something I found difficult to comprehend initially, but with me studying as well, it made it easier to come to terms with."

It was that thirst for new experiences, after bowing out at Arsenal Ladies following a win against Everton to retain the FA Women's Cup, that gave Kerr the extra edge when she was interviewed for the Stirling job. The former centre back had stacked up plenty of experience as a coach, having managed at Kilmarnock and Hibernian Ladies, as well as holding a UEFA Pro Licence, but she didn't want to rest on her CV to get her next opportunity.

Although Kerr admits that she's never been somebody to set herself career goals – "it's very difficult to plan ahead in sport because it's so competitive" – an ambition to test herself in men's football has always been present. So when the university gave her the chance to take the reins of their team, it was the perfect opportunity to scratch that itch.

"My first coaching job back in 1989 was for an under-11 boys' team and I've worked at all stages of the pathway, so that was quite important to me," she says.

"It's about getting the right opportunity, but I was never averse to saying I wanted to work here or there. I had aspirations to work in the men's game and to achieve things in the women's game as well.

"In terms of team dynamics, there is a difference in my opinion. The way I would summarise it is that men are easier to manage than women because there is less emotion involved with working with a male group. In terms of the decision-making process, it only affects one individual, whereas with a women's team, a decision can have an impact on more than just one of the team. In terms of coaching, women are probably more receptive, but I don't know the reason for that."

As well as getting the opportunity to broaden her skills working with different gender teams, Kerr's role at Stirling University has provided exposure to other elite sports. While higher-education football is still a relatively untapped market for professional clubs, Kerr says that working alongside a variety of top coaches means her players get more well-rounded training plans.

"It's a breath of fresh air to work alongside coaches from other sports because you learn heaps, especially when you come from a football background," Kerr adds.

"When you come from such a high-profile sport, you can overlook what other sports are doing. My time at university has given me the chance to look at what the golf, swimming and tennis coaches are doing. That's really good and it's exciting to be in that environment."

All of that experience can be seen in the way Kerr leads her team. Throughout the match against East Kilbride, she's engaged in the play and always trying to pass on advice from the touchline. In the dressing room, she's firm but fair with the players and even tries to offer nuggets of coaching advice during the brief half-time interval.

Unfortunately, today's result doesn't match the preparation Kerr and Stirling have put in. In what was probably their most difficult match of the season, the runaway leaders put the students to the sword – scoring four goals in a rampant second-half performance to take all three points. After witnessing Kerr's softer side throughout the match, when the dressing room door shuts at full-time, the sound of raised voices and expletives can be heard peppering the air as I wait outside to speak to her.

"It's not normally like that," Kerr tells me when she finally emerges. "But sometimes we've got to tell them and today was one of those times."

While her gender might steal the headlines, it's Kerr's varied experience that makes her approach so effective as a coach. If she's enjoying success in the dugout of a men's team, why doesn't she think that more of the top female managers are making the jump across the gender codes?

"I don't know the figures, but I'd think there are very few female coaches who apply for jobs [in the men's game] in the first place," she answers. "What the reasons are, I can't really comment, but this is the only job I've applied for. The very fact that what I'm doing is an isolated case in the UK suggests that maybe there's not an interest from females who are qualified and also that clubs haven't approached certain individuals.

"I don't think managing in the men's game is in everybody's plans. Some female coaches of the right level won't want to work in the men's game, but there will be some who do. If they've got the qualifications and skillset, then why shouldn't they?"

Kerr might be carrying the torch for others to follow in the UK, but she's not alone as a pioneer when you start looking further afield. Across the English Channel, Frenchwoman Corinne Diacre was appointed manager at Ligue 2 side Clermont Foot in the same summer as Kerr started her role, while 28-year-old Chan Yeun-ting hit the headlines in 2016 after guiding Eastern Sports Club to the Hong Kong Premier League title.

If there is to be an influx of female coaches infiltrating the British game over the next few years, then Kerr – and Stirling – will be at the forefront of that revolution. While her appointment grabbed some attention at first, it didn't lead to any change elsewhere in Britain, but Kerr is happy to be a trailblazer. Even if she's a bit unsure about the tag.

"I just see myself as an ordinary coach and person, without taking gender into it. I'm a coach working hard to get better and help the players I work with – whoever that might be," she adds, before leaving the ground.

"If the job I'm doing helps others, then fantastic. I'm always here to give advice to anyone who wants to get into coaching, male or female. Do I see myself as a role model? I suppose I do, but then I think that's just me as a person."

IN BED WITH MARADONA

It's midway through the second half and Dapo Afolayan is limbering up on the touchline. The teenager is decked out in a Solihull Moors' yellow-and-blue-striped shirt for the first time and is primed to make his debut.

It's only been a few days since Afolayan, a first-year student at Loughborough, swapped the Scholars for the National League. Now, standing next to the fourth official waiting to be introduced in front of several hundred supporters, the forward is set for his sink-or-swim moment.

Afolayan has stepped up four divisions to join Solihull. And with mostly professional outfits competing alongside the Moors in English football's fifth tier, it's a jump of great magnitude. But as Afolayan readies himself to enter the fray against Sutton United, he shows no sign of nerves. Instead, he waits at the edge of the pitch, eyes focused on the stage where his performance is set to take place. As the board goes up to show the number 17, Afolayan takes one last intake of breath and runs out on to the Damson Parkway pitch.

The myth goes that when Diego Maradona pulled on the shirt of Argentinos for his maiden senior match, his first action was to wow the crowd by poking a delicate nutmeg through the legs of a more experienced opponent. And while Afolayan can't claim to have pulled off such a precocious move on his Solihull bow, his first touch still had quite an impact.

Minutes after taking to the pitch, the wiry youngster is on the move:

scampering from the halfway line with little more than clear space in front of him. To his right, fellow debutant and Charlton Athletic loanee Regan Charles-Cook is streaking away down the wing and spots Afolayan's run as he approaches the edge of the box. Waiting just long enough to draw the last remaining Sutton defender away from Afolayan, Charles-Cook pulls a low cross back into the student's path. The goal is at his mercy.

Afolayan takes his time, plants his left foot into the turf beneath him and calmly rolls a side-footed effort past the diving goalkeeper and into the net. As cool as you like, the composed teen nonchalantly jogs towards his new adoring fans, before turning back to celebrate with Charles-Cook.

It's that sort of level-headed maturity that led to Afolayan being here today. It's a tag he's been carrying ever since the promising starlet left Chelsea's youth team as a 14-year-old and swapped his attention to forging a completely different career path.

"At the time, it was hard to give up Chelsea," Afolayan recalls of the decision that set him on his way to that dream debut for Solihull, not to mention a heap of textbooks at Loughborough.

"The reason I left was I'd have needed to leave school to carry on there. When they introduced category academies, it meant players couldn't stay at school to be part of it — I was supposed to be doing my GCSEs the year after and I wasn't happy to only learn three days a week.

"It seems that a lot of people sack off their education at a young age and don't think about going to university, which is why it's rare to find an 18-year-old footballer who has got A levels."

With the bright lights of the Premier League – and the fame and riches that brings – dangled in front of teenagers who want nothing more than to play football for a living, it's easy to see why Afolayan's choice to opt out of Chelsea's youth system is an exception. But guided by the advice of his parents, the Londoner knuckled down and got the grades he needed to enrol for a three-year civil engineering degree at Loughborough. And while the football-mad 19-year-old admits that the university's reputation for sport helped bring him to Leicestershire, he has no regrets about his decision to turn his back on Stamford Bridge, despite embarking on a route that's considered less than ordinary for most footballers.

"That's mainly down to how we treat youth football in England," he says wisely. "We say to children that there is one path to football: you work hard, go to an academy and get a scholarship. Then you get a pro contract and try to get in the first team.

"You don't hear that you don't need to be in an academy at eight- or nine-years old, and that you can play in the park and get spotted. There are lots of people in academies at a young age who get released, don't play for a couple of years, then make it all the way to the Premier League – you're not told that though.

"That's why people don't think about going to university. It isn't an option for many because, once you're in an academy or become a scholar, you fast-track school.

"From a young age, my parents told me how important education is and that it's the one thing nobody can take away from you. I always bought into that. I understand where they're coming from, having seen friends and people around me going through situations – it shows that education really helps. I have friends who have been playing football and got injured, then they're not left with much."

After boldly leaving Chelsea in favour of education, it's no real surprise that Afolayan's next move after completing his GCSEs wasn't to simply get on with his A levels at his local sixth form. Instead, he left English shores for a part of the world that has embraced the union between sport and grades for decades. A two-year stint living in Toronto didn't dampen Afolayan's love for football, even though the Canadian national sport of ice hockey is more likely to dominate the sports headlines over there than the beautiful game.

Once he and his family had settled into their new home – and the then-16-year-old had joined Ontario High School – Afolayan was quick to scout out where he could get out on the pitch. While he studied for the high school diploma that would earn him the qualifications to come back to Britain and go to university, he turned out for Major League Soccer (MLS) side Toronto FC's reserve team.

While it offered Afolayan exposure to the North American system and experience of playing men's football at such a young age, there weren't the same depth of opportunities to make the jump to becoming a professional as there are in England. As with a lot of elite American sport, it's boom or bust for many young footballers – and those who fail to make the elite level are often left with nothing to fall back on. So, once more, Afolayan turned his back on convention and switched continents again to join up with Loughborough University.

"It's not really a big change for me and the Loughborough programme is very good," Afolayan explains.

"After living abroad, I know about lots of other programmes in the States and Canada, and this is similar. It's the closest thing in the UK to the heavily funded programmes in the States. I've got friends who go to University of Carolina and other universities out there, and they get their degree funded for them. They train just as much and the only difference is they do a few more gym sessions than us.

"I felt like I needed to be at home for football. The one thing the MLS is lacking is their youth system because it's not as thought through as in other countries. I have a lot of friends who are trying to play football professionally in the States, but it's so hard for them – the introduction of the USL Pro League means a lot of people don't go to uni because, if you do, you don't get the same chances to move on.

"It's a big commitment and, for me, it's not worth that. I've had friends who have tried and not made it [as a pro], then it's a long way back."

It seems that even at such a young age, Afolayan is picking a way through the minefield of professional football to reach his Mecca. He's avoiding the possible pitfalls that others have come across on the way towards his goal, while giving himself a platform to fall back on if he doesn't realise his dreams.

While his spell playing for Loughborough in regional non-league might only have lasted a matter of months, his focus is to complete all three years at university to get a good degree. In the months since Afolayan broke into the Scholars first team, I heard of several Football League clubs who had made enquiries about the forward, but despite a week's trial at League One Rochdale shortly before signing for Solihull, the flexibility of part-time football fitted best with university life. It also means he can still benefit from Loughborough's performance regime while turning out for the Moors in the Conference.

"Being part-time makes it easier for me," Afolayan says. "It means I can go to lectures in the day and shoot down to training in the evening. A lot of the boys at Solihull work as well, so it's a good set-up for them too.

"Liam [McDonald, Solihull's manager] understands how much education means to me and works around it. I don't know if the move would have gone through without him – he's good to me and is always there to help me out.

"I've got two years left at Loughborough and the arrangement suits me perfectly at the moment. I train with Loughborough on Monday and Tuesday, if there isn't a game, then train with Solihull on Thursday and play at the weekend. I can make it work as long as I stay focused.

"When I was at Rochdale, I didn't feel out of place at all, so I know I can play higher, it's just up to me to prove that. Working alongside full-time football would be difficult though. I'm just trying to get my head down and make sure I'm working towards something for the next couple of years."

The move to Solihull has gone some way to vindicating Afolayan's career choices and not just because of his early stand-out performances in the blue and yellow. When he joined up with his new teammates at the West Midlands club, he came across a couple of familiar faces from his Chelsea days. Goalkeeper Nathan Baker is currently on loan at the Moors from Stamford Bridge, while Ghanaian defender Nortei Nortey has been bouncing around non-league since his release from West London a few years ago.

It shows that while many might have seen Afolayan's refusal to prioritise his place in Chelsea's youth team above all else as a backwards step, he's no further behind others who stayed on. In fact, he believes that already having a host of appearances for senior teams further down the leagues has been more beneficial than kicking his heels in a Premier League under-23s division.

"For the players in my age group, I think a couple are out on loan, but the rest are playing 23s football," Afolayan explains.

"It doesn't prepare you for professional football and it's like playing in an academy. The difference between that and men's football is huge, and that's one thing that's helped me a lot because I've been playing men's football since I was 16. People are more experienced and do different things, but in 23s football, it's always against similar players on nice pitches.

"Solihull played at Woking recently and, I kid you not, half the pitch was like a beach. It had been waterlogged and they just whacked loads of sand on it: we walked out before the game and could have been wearing flip-flops. I don't know many 23s teams who would have played on pitches like that. You've just got to get on with it sometimes.

"To me, that's all part of my learning curve. If you start at the top and move down, rather than starting from the bottom, you appreciate it more."

While Afolayan is already starting to make an impact at Solihull, his next test might be to stay focused on his civil engineering degree if he attracts anymore interest from professional clubs higher up the ranks. What would he do if he had to make a choice between education and football?

"Football has always been a big part of my life and giving that up would be hard – I don't think I could do it. But I know education is important and will open doors for me," Afolayan answers, noticeably straining at the prospect of choosing one over the other.

"When I finish my degree I'll be 21 and will be able to play football for however long I want, but then I'll also have the degree to help me get jobs in the future too. If I had to give one up, I don't which one it would be – I couldn't answer that.

"I've got two years left at university, but if something comes up, I'd have to talk it through with my family. At the moment, I'm just going to take it as it is, then if something happens, I'll have to make a decision about what's best for me."

As Afolayan makes his own unique route up the football ladder with Loughborough's help, he's not the only student who is using the university as a stepping stone to a brighter future.

THE CAMPUS CHAMPIONS

When Matt Reeves entered a lecture theatre at Loughborough University for the first time, there was nothing to suspect it would be his first step towards becoming a Premier League champion.

The teenager was a full back of little reputation. Having been released by Fulham's academy, he was just another youngster with a tale of rejection to tell. So when he came on to campus on that early spring day, soaking up the surroundings that would form part of his new home, it's no surprise that the awe he felt looking at the university's sports facilities has stuck with him. The Kent-born youngster had decided this small market town in Leicestershire was the perfect tonic to deal with the disappointment of being shown the door at Craven Cottage. But he could have had no idea where it would eventually lead him.

"It got to the point where I was making a decision between A levels and university or going down the professional football route," recalls Reeves, with only a hint of the southern lilt that accompanied him as he started his maiden term at Loughborough.

"I'd always enjoyed school to an extent and did quite well, so I wanted to pursue that a bit more – and there was no better option than Loughborough. It had a great reputation, not only for a sports and exercise degree but also for the quality of their sports teams because I was hoping to carry on playing while I studied."

Reeves' ambitions of playing in Loughborough's first team didn't start too well though. As the new season began in his first year at uni, the full back wasn't anywhere near the performance squad and had to take the long way round to reach the starting XI. It took an astute first-team coach to spot Reeves playing in one of the university's other teams before he got his chance to shine. Although once he got the opportunity, he soon established himself as a permanent fixture in the side.

While Reeves had all but given up on his hopes of playing professional football before enrolling at Loughborough, it was a twist of fate triggered by his inclusion in the Scholars squad that opened the door to his new career.

After arriving on campus early to join pre-season training before his final year as a student, Reeves received an invite to visit Leicester City's training ground for a trial. But there'd be no need for his football boots this time – it was his ability as a junior sports scientist that was under the microscope.

"I'll always say that I was extremely lucky at the time," Reeves admits humbly. "I was preparing to go back for pre-season with the Loughborough University team ahead of my final year, but campus didn't tend to get busy when the students were away, so I was at a bit of a loose end.

"I decided to start thinking about my career, so I sent off a couple of emails to the local Midlands clubs, one of which was Leicester. Sure enough, Dave Rennie, the physio who's been there for years, replied to me quite quickly and offered me the chance to go in for the day in a shadowing kind of role. For me, that was great and a really good opportunity – I didn't think twice about it."

One day's work experience turned to two, then a week. Before Reeves knew it, he was being offered an internship and was helping out at the Foxes' Belvoir Drive training ground three times a week, as well as supporting the back-room staff on home match days at the 32,000-capacity King Power Stadium. It was the dream scenario for an ambitious student and gave Reeves an invaluable insight into the inner workings of a professional football club, albeit one in a state of flux when he first arrived in 2008.

Having been relegated into English football's third tier for the first time in their history, the Foxes had just appointed Nigel Pearson as manager. Pearson was a man who had earned promising reviews in short spells in charge at Carlisle United and Southampton, and had also gathered a lot of knowledge from a stint working with England's under-21 side, for who he became the first manager to lead an English national side out at the new Wembley.

There was a lot of work to do. So when Pearson started his new role, one of the first things he did was to overhaul match preparation and install a new ethos towards sports science. Reeves was in the prime position to benefit and was given a permanent deal following his graduation.

"You can learn a lot of theoretical aspects in books and lectures, but putting things into practice is very different," Reeves says.

"After I went full-time, we set up an understanding between Leicester City and Loughborough that would benefit both parties. Sure enough, we got some students who came in to get good experience at Leicester and we tapped into lecturers at the university.

"At the end of that season, Nigel and I, along with some of the other staff, went to Hull City for 18 months, which meant the understanding with the university went on the back burner for a bit – although when we came back in December 2011, we re-established those links."

It was Pearson's homecoming that heralded another upturn in Leicester's fortunes. The return to the King Power Stadium of the former manager and his back-room team, including Reeves, saw the Blues challenge for promotion back to the Premier League for the first time in a decade. One failed play-off attempt later and Leicester were back among the big boys for the start of the 2014-15 season and after languishing at the foot of the table for most of the season, went on an incredible winning run to secure their safety against the odds. While Pearson left the club under a cloud at the end of that season, Reeves stayed on as head of fitness & conditioning and so formed part of an even more incredible underdog story – one that will be repeatedly told by generations of football managers as inspiration that every dog (or fox) could have its day.

While Jamie Vardy, Riyad Mahrez and co earned the headlines as Leicester stunned the recognised order to clinch an unbelievable first Premier League title, Reeves was pivotal in keeping the Foxes' stars in peak condition for the run-in. Not that he's taking much credit for it.

"It's all been a great experience, but we can't really take much credit for that," Reeves counters when I suggest how important his sport science team's role must have been in the Championship win.

"A lot of people asked us as the season went on if we were nervous, if we thought the players could keep it up or if their legs would go towards the end of the season. We had belief in what we were trying to achieve and that there was a plan to it: it was probably similar to what we'd done in previous seasons.

"It was very difficult to keep up that run of form and keep getting the wins, especially when the pressure built. But from a physical point of view, we were quite happy with things.

"Our job as sports scientists, fitness coaches and the medical department is to make sure we have as many of the first-team squad available for the manager to pick as possible. That not only means getting the same team out on a Saturday, but also that players are available for training throughout the week so that if the manager needs to do some tactical work, the players he needs are fit and available to be on the training pitch."

While Reeves remains modest about his impact on Leicester's miracle season, one of the pillars to his side's success was undoubtedly manager Claudio Ranieri's ability to pick a consistent and settled team throughout the entire season. In fact, after a gruelling nine-month season, it was the Foxes who had made the fewest team changes in the league throughout the 38 matches, only highlighting further just how important Reeves and his team's work was.

The triumph meant that, less than a decade after sending those hopeful emails from student digs during a non-league club's pre-season training camp, Reeves was sitting on the bench in the Champions League. It was a baptism of fire, with an extra challenge to juggle European commitments with defending their title. They were new pressures for Reeves, but not something any of his fellow Loughborough alumni hadn't handled before.

○○○○

A 100-mile drive down the usually congested M1 and there's a man who knows all too well what it's like to balance the delicate scales of success. Although Reeves's glory at Leicester came as a surprise, Chelsea first-team fitness coach Chris Jones is used to working in an environment where achievement is only measured in silverware.

Jones graduated 10 years before Reeves donned his cap and gown, and after landing a job in Chelsea's academy in 2006, was promoted to the first team to work under Carlo Ancelotti three years later – and he's been there ever since. It's meant that Jones has sampled life under a host of super-coaches, including Jose Mourinho, Guus Hiddink and now Antonio Conte. But whoever has been in charge, the task is always the same: win trophies. Although for all of the three Premier League titles and FA Cups the Blues have won in Jones's time at the club, one gong stands out above the rest.

"It has to be the Champions League [in 2012] because it was such a wild year," Jones recalls.

"We started off the season with AVB [Andre Villas-Boas] and it didn't turn out as well as we'd have liked, but Steve Holland, Eddie Newton, Roberto Di Matteo and I were thrown together to muddle through and pick up the pieces to get the most out of the group, which was not in a wonderful state.

"We had to find a way to get them to refocus on what we had to do. It was a bit of a journey really – we had the FA Cup final one week and then the Champions League final the week after.

"It's hard to do Premier League, FA Cup and Champions League, so the games needed to be plotted through carefully, deciding which team were going to play which game. For example, we played Arsenal at the Emirates the weekend before we had Barcelona away on the Wednesday. We had to make changes for the Arsenal game and take players off at the right time so they could be ready for Wednesday – it was a tough time.

"While we use GPS and heart-rate monitors, it's not just a case of punching an equation into a computer and getting the answer you need. You have to talk to the players and look at them to see who can do or deal with what. It's more the craft side of it."

As much as intuition develops over time, so does the technology. When Jones first started learning his trade at Loughborough back in the mid-90s, sports science in football was in its earliest forms ("Back in the 90s, GPS was just something the armed forces used," Jones explains), it has now blossomed into something that has infiltrated almost every facet of the modern game.

So with the university at the forefront of the new revolution when sports science took the national game by storm, it's no surprise that Jones, and Reeves, are far from the only Loughborough graduates who are part of a secret network of former students throughout English football. At almost every club, there is somebody within the coaching team who spent time getting a qualification in Leicestershire. Most notably, Manchester City's Head of Performance Sam Erith and Manchester United's Head of Athletic Development Tony Strudwick are others who have also gone on to become Premier League champions with their clubs.

"Loughborough was the platform," Jones adds. "It's amazing to think of all the Loughborough lads from roughly the same era who are surrounding me in the Premier League – it's just incredible really.

"It's not as if it's jobs for the boys. You don't survive in any industry, particularly football, by not being good enough. You'd be out within two weeks if you're not up to it, so I don't believe there's any favouritism or university bond; it's just a big pool of lads who have kicked on for whatever reason and have talent in that area.

"It's funny; I sometimes look back to when I was at Loughborough and thought the world was so open, which is the beauty of being young. You don't have any pressures thinking I need to do that or what job will I get. It's brilliant what I've been able to do, the places I've been and the people I've worked with. To compare with back then, I'd think: 'wow, this is great – what a way to go with work'. Hopefully, it's not done yet."

The razzmatazz of the Premier League isn't for everyone though and while the list of Loughborough graduates earning positions at top clubs seemingly grows by the season, one alumni has been absent for a number of years.

○○○○

When I call Dan Harris to talk to him about his unusual decision to jump out of British football and head to the Far East to get his kicks, I'm welcomed with a burst of lively K-pop music instead of the more traditional rings.

"I have people from around the world calling me, agents and players, and every single person hammers me for the dial tone they hear when they ring me," the Londoner laughs after answering my call.

"When I first came to Korea, I was given a phone number with the same last four digits I used in the UK. It had been allocated to somebody else previously who had cancelled their contract and I couldn't change the ringtone. Now I hear this rascal K-pop music whenever someone calls me – it's not really in keeping with someone who tries to keep a low profile."

Harris is friendly and chatty, and can't wait to start talking about his career change. A move that many established home-grown coaches bouncing around the world's most-renowned league wouldn't have given a second thought to. But after stints at several top British clubs, including West Brom and Celtic, Harris needed a change of scenery.

After two years out of the game following his departure from Parkhead, Harris was hopping on a plane to discuss a new project. The only hitch: it was in South Korea, which was 5,300 miles away from his family home and at a club that had no history and no players. If there was ever any doubt whether Harris's move to new K-League franchise Seoul E-Land would be a success though, the fact that he's talking to me from South Korea's capital three years on gives its own empathic answer.

"It was a tough sell," Harris admits, thinking back to the conversation he had with his wife to float the idea of moving continents. "When I sat down and spoke to my wife, we had to find South Korea on the map first. She was really supportive and we decided it was the right thing to do for the family.

"I'd been out to meet the chief executive and other directors. I had 27 hours in Seoul and we packed a lot in. In that time, I got a chance to find out what the club was about. We thought, why not go to a whole new culture and give it a try? And we're still here now."

Harris had turned down several enticing offers south of the border after leaving Celtic and chose instead to take stock of where his career was headed. The whirlwind of British football goes at one hundred miles an hour and the time spent away from regular work served as extra perspective for the Loughborough graduate. He travelled the globe, learning from other coaches in other cultures and sports, and recognised the value of looking further afield for his next job, rather than making the more obvious move to another British club. Harris yearned for more than just the kudos of coaching in the most high-profile league on the planet; he wanted a project he could get stuck in to for the long term – and being number-two in Seoul ticked that box.

"It's become a transient game, particularly in the UK, which creates the disconnect between clubs and fans," Harris explains. "It's a bit mercenary. For me, I want to do it the other way and really commit to the club I'm at, then I see how the cards fall from there.

"You do need to be savvy to make sure you make the right choices, but people in the game can soon see if you're in it for the wrong reasons. The money and fame can't be the driving force: you've got to be in this game because you love it and want to push yourself.

"We're fortunate to be from a magnificent country that has a great love for football, but the nature of it means it can get a bit insular or lazy in the sense that we think because we're the most popular football nation in the world, we've got everything sorted. For me it's great, but I wanted to go off and learn about sports, people and nations.

"There are a lot of opportunities abroad, especially outside of Europe, at the moment. That's because the British game is, rightly or wrongly, held up on a pedestal. One of the fears is the sense of being out of sight, out of mind – once you go abroad and leave the media maelstrom in England, you can drop off the radar a bit. If you go abroad, it's not necessarily a stepping stone back to England, which is what other coaches are wary of."

For Harris, packing his family and career off to South Korea was the next leg of an education that had been growing since he started at Loughborough in 1998. When he signed up for the sports science degree that would eventually open doors for him as a graduate, Harris freely admits he found himself in the right place at the right time to succeed.

With the first shoots of sports science appearing in the British game before the turn of the millennium, Harris and his classmates were at the forefront of a new revolution. Previously, clubs and players had given little credence to the idea of sports nutrition, preparation and recovery, but now a new breed were teaching new lessons.

One of the first big research projects that Harris remembers working on at Loughborough was the basis of Lucozade Sport's famous 33% longer campaign, which was fronted by England captain Alan Shearer on a treadmill, announcing the sports drink's powers of stamina compared to water. While the trials were all used as a powerful marketing tool, which helped Lucozade become the huge brand it is today, Harris and his cohorts were the students doing the initial number crunching.

While Harris's career blossomed as sports science became a more respected part of the game, he still remembers facing some cynicism when he and other Loughborough students were sent out to talk about how nutrition could play a key role in young pros' development.

"The first few times we went into clubs, we were facing a fairly hostile audience," he recalls. "The mass of that hostility was coming from the coaching staff because the perception was that we were bringing in some sort of dark art from a mumbo-jumbo background. There was a lack of understanding about what it was we were there to do.

"As soon as you take the ego away and people realise you're there to help them, you're fishing in more fertile ground.

"Sadly, there is still an element of wariness and cynicism today because there are some people who have come into the game and let sports science down because they didn't understand the game enough. In order to help someone improve, you've got to have a real decent understanding of the game – just because something is old-fashioned, doesn't make it wrong.

"For me, the data and the science should always underpin the coach's eyes, it should never replace them. There are a lot of spreadsheet warriors in the game, but it's still about people and players."

In South Korea, Harris is again working in a developing football country and playing his part to improve the national game while aiming to bring success on the pitch for Seoul E-Land. In the five years since he last worked in British football, the game has continued to morph beyond recognition of the 90s era when Harris first started at Loughborough. But from the outside looking in, where does he see the next stage of development coming from?

"There's still an area to focus on in sports psychology and that's where I think the next wave of progress is going to come from," Harris considers.

"Ultimately, this is a mental game and it's about being able to handle pressure. The area that is going to see the biggest advance now is psychological preparation of players – there's no doubt we can still get better at that in England.

"Now English football has become about asset management: how can you get the absolute most from everyone and help them reach their potential? When you look at the Leicester City model when they won the Premier League, they had the perfect storm of helping every single player and member of staff squeeze every last drop of potential out of themselves. As a unit, they achieved something nobody thought was possible. That has got to be the model for everyone moving forward."

As each of the three Loughborough graduates would attest, if there's a blueprint to follow for getting success, starting off in Leicestershire is a pretty good idea.

SPRING OF CHANGE

The green shoots of spring normally provide new hope. A fresh sense of being and promise. But as the first signs emerge that winter is ending, the changes coming to Loughborough only spread concern.

Just over a month earlier, the horizon had looked much brighter. A stronger than expected Christmas period had seen the Scholars pick up some crucial points to pull away from the congested pack of relegation candidates at the foot of the Midland Premier Division. Loughborough were heading for mid-table security, while they were among the favourites to win the BUCS Championship after topping the northern division.

It promised to be an exciting few months ahead as the students returned to campus, although the reality was somewhat different. With the exception of the victory against Durham that saw them clinch the D-day bragging rights in early February, Loughborough's students found the winning feeling hard to come by.

A run of seven matches without a win saw the side tumble back down towards the league's trapdoor, leaving them within a point of the dreaded relegation zone. And while previous spells of bad form had been justified by progress in BUCS competition, even that grain of hope had been washed away following a disastrous quarter-final tie with Cardiff Metropolitan University.

I hadn't been able to make the Wednesday afternoon fixture against the Archers, but as I followed the match on Twitter, I could scarcely believe my eyes as the BUCS campaign that had appeared to be heading for an exciting climax unravelled in a series of 140-character bursts.

Cardiff were always going to provide tough opposition, with their own student side performing admirably in their first-ever campaign in the Welsh Premier Division. But with many of their first teamers being used to maintain their good performance in the senior ranks, Loughborough were the most likely victors as they took to the field.

After half an hour of almost constant refreshing Loughborough Football's Twitter page on my laptop, the first notification finally popped up. And it was bad news: 'Goal for @CardiffMetFC as the number four heads in from a corner'.

Just as I began to lament the same issue that has blighted Loughborough so many times before, another post popped up: 'Two goals in three minutes for @CardiffMetFC as the number 10 chips over the keeper'. I sank in my chair and decided it was best that I turned my attention elsewhere. From a young age, I – just like many other sports fans – always had a suspicion that I somehow controlled the fortunes of my favourite team simply with my actions or thoughts. So I'd have to put Loughborough's match to the back of my mind and hope that with my focus turned elsewhere, they would right the wrongs I had done by sticking too closely to social media.

When I checked again shortly after the beginning of the second half, my irrational beliefs appeared to have had the desired effect. Two goals for Loughborough, through Ben Last and Drew Bridge, had levelled things up, although Cardiff had struck again before half-time to retake the lead at 3-2. Once more, another new post had appeared at the top of the page. No harm in pressing it. After all, my notion that the world somehow revolved around my every more is just misplaced human narcissism, right? It seems not. 'Loughborough have a man sent off, down to 10' read the Twitter feed. Then moments later, another one: 'Loughborough down to nine as James Stallan picks up a second yellow card'. This time that was proof enough that I'm cursed. I pressed the little red cross at the top of the window and left the match behind, knowing that I'd almost certainly done irreparable damage now. When I logged back on a while later, it was official: Loughborough had lost 4-3 and were out. All ambitions of glory extinguished for good.

If the downturn in results wasn't enough of a concern, the defeat to Cardiff Met also meant the end of another key figure's time at Loughborough. If Dapo Afolayan's transfer to Solihull had left a notable hole in the starting XI, the announcement that Michael Skubala was leaving his role as performance manager left a crater in the Scholars' coaching team.

A few weeks earlier, Skubala was unveiled as England's new futsal head coach and elite performance manager for the sport. And although the 34-year-old had agreed to stay on at the university until this season's BUCS campaign had ended, the premature defeat to their Welsh counterparts heralded an abrupt end to his tenure. There would be no blaze of glory this time. BUCS first-team coach Ackerley would pick up the reins left by Skubala until the end of the season. But as the Scholars gave their outgoing performance manager a send-off, the true impact of Skubala's departure was sure to be felt.

OOOO

When your country comes calling, it's hard to turn it down. So when Skubala received a message from the FA to say he'd been chosen to lead the nation's futsal programme, his response was always going to be positive. He'd been combining his work at Loughborough with his role as head coach of England futsal's under-23 side for a while, so when the job came up, Skubala was in the box seat to get it. With a full complement of futsal and football coaching badges, and as one of the nation's most well-rounded coaches, he was the perfect fit to grow the sport. And boy do England need it.

Languishing below football minnows such as the Solomon Islands, Georgia and Vietnam, England's futsal team lie 62nd in FIFA's world rankings. And with the techniques developed by playing the small-sided indoor sport lauded as key skills to creating some of the most-gifted international footballers currently lighting up the planet, it's a concerning trend. So while all the attention shines on England manager Gareth Southgate and his seemingly thankless quest to lead the Three Lions back to the summit of the world game, it could be Skubala's appointment that has the biggest long-term impact on that mission.

"There is an argument – that I'm not totally sure about – that teams will never win a football World Cup unless they play futsal properly," Skubala tells me, shortly after his appointment.

"But if you look at the countries who play it well, you can understand it. The top six football nations in the world are all in the top 10 for futsal as well. They all have developed futsal programmes in their schools and leagues, but we're light years behind as a football nation because we've got this stiff upper lip about getting players outside on the grass.

"Futsal probably does have a bigger impact on football than people realise. In some ways, this is probably a job that could impact football in a bigger way than a lot of other jobs in the sport.

"I was talking to somebody the other day who even said that mine was probably the most important appointment for football in this country for the past 20 years. He said that if we can get futsal right, I could be the one that wins the World Cup for England – not Gareth Southgate."

While the illusions of grandeur might sound tantalising, the reality is considerably further away from idle talk of World Cup victories. Skubala's appointment might be a step in the right direction as the FA's first full-time staffer charged solely with increasing futsal's presence in England, but as many have found previously, overhauling a long-standing football culture isn't so easy.

Skubala's first challenge is to raise awareness of a sport that most mainstream football fans in Britain have only a fleeting knowledge of, despite its huge popularity across the rest of the world. Then once he's achieved that, the target is to convince schools, football clubs and other organisations that less time spent on a traditional football pitch and more on an indoor futsal court is the right way to go. It's an uphill task, but Skubala is sure he can achieve his goals. After all, he's grown used to fighting the cause of an unheralded football programme that does things a little bit differently.

"I've always been really passionate about what Loughborough do and in some aspects the futsal elite performance manager role is similar," he reasons.

"It's a similar challenge because football clubs don't engage with Loughborough due to not knowing about them or about the level the university are playing at. When we got players coming to Loughborough they'd say: 'blimey, we're from Rochdale in League One and you've got better facilities than we have'.

"It's similar with futsal. Loughborough have set me up for the job quite nicely by not being in the pro game and less funded, so we have to think about things in a different way to develop internally."

Futsal's status in the British professional game is barely worthy of mention, particularly among the top home-grown managers. As I chat to Skubala about the current state of the sport, he can name only Bournemouth's Eddie Howe as an example of an English manager who understands the merits of using futsal properly as part of the south-coast club's academy system. It's a galling realisation, especially when you consider many of the Premier League's top foreign bosses, including Roberto Martinez and Mauricio Pochettino, are thought to be big advocates of the game in the way they set up tactically. It's not just our players who are being left behind.

When I quiz Skubala about examples that highlight the use of futsal in the full-sized game, he can't help but gush with an extensive list.

"When Ronaldinho scored with that toe poke for Barcelona against Chelsea in 2005, he was using a futsal technique," Skubala explains excitedly. "In playing the game, he's gone to his default setting to quickly get a shot off and it's something he's learned through playing futsal as a youngster in Brazil.

"When you watch Brazil or Spain play, you think they're creating these openings off the cuff, but instead they're calling on experience they've learned as part of their make-up as players. So when they do play, it's not really off the cuff, it's through futsal and coaching because it has been a heavy part of their development.

"The ball at the top level of futsal moves seven times faster than it does in football. That means the Spanish can get through a defensive block because if they haven't got the space, they've learned how to get past that, whereas England can't get through a block. We think we can do it, but we're not trained to as kids.

"Conversely, when you talk about pressing, futsal players do it a lot quicker than others because it's a technique that comes from playing the sport. Iceland, for example, have a strong indoor futsal programme, so when they blocked out England to beat them in the Euros, it was no real surprise because they have defenders who learned how to do that through futsal."

Just spending a short time with Skubala is enough to feel his fervour for futsal and it becomes even clearer why he felt he had to trade in life at Loughborough for his new position at St. George's Park. Skubala told me earlier in the season that his dream move would be to become a club's director of football, but I get the impression that shaping an entire nation's perception of futsal might just have trumped that.

Participation is the first hurdle to jump though. While the highest-profile English player to have used futsal as part of his development is Watford's Will Hughes, who has played his entire career in the second tier, very few of the next wave of teenagers aiming to make a breakthrough have proper experience of the game. While the FA's National Futsal League is made up of part-time teams, including Loughborough University, the story is different away from our shores. In Italy, there are more registered futsal players than footballers and in countries such as Iran, there are an abundance of professional clubs to join.

"It's a tough job and it is really daunting," Skubala admits. "A lot of the National League futsal clubs are heavily foreign-influenced and players don't get paid. If a player drops out of a pro club as a 16-year-old and is offered a few quid to play for a non-league club, he's much more likely to do that than play futsal, even though it's possible to make a career in futsal.

"I played international futsal and went around the world with it – it has taken me to about 50 countries. We currently have three Englishmen who have gone on to be professional futsal players abroad: one of them is in Spain and living the dream, one is in Croatia and playing in front of 3,000 people each week, and the other is in Italy. Just because you can't play professionally here, doesn't mean you can't do it elsewhere."

As Skubala gets down to work, his focus is on smaller targets. By increasing participation among the younger age groups, he hopes to encourage more players to continue past their 16th birthday and teach the next generation of footballers important lessons from the court. And if those playing numbers go up, then better performances in international competitions, possibly in the 11-a-side game as well as futsal itself, will hopefully follow hot on the heels. One thing's for sure, there's unlikely to be any great turnaround overnight.

"Success would be people understanding properly what futsal is. We need people to understand it not only as a development, but as a sport in its own right," Skubala adds. "What the FA has realised over the past six months is that there is a place for futsal, but they didn't have the expertise in there. Currently, the maximum ranking we could achieve with an England futsal team that is really good is 40 in the world.

"Previously, we thought we had good footballers here, so we could do well at this indoor game – like we'll just put a team out and we'll do well. But over the past 10 years, we've been battered and bruised, and realised that approach isn't working because the game is too good. Hopefully, this is the start of the change."

OOOO

The weekend after the BUCS defeat that spelled the end of Skubala's time with Loughborough, the Scholars travelled to Sutton Coldfield to face

Boldmere St. Michaels in a crunch Midland Premier Division match.

The Mikes were in the middle of a three-match winning run that had seen them start their own ascent past Loughborough in the league table and away from the relegation zone. They were a side that had been battling for survival for most of the season, while the students were fast looking like the side that perennially gets dragged into a scrap at the bottom after looking safe in mid-table.

By half-time, those stereotypes appeared to have been turned on their head. Goals from Drew Bridge and Joe Jackson had given the visitors a commanding 2-0 lead at the break, with the students confidently showing that now the focus was solely on the non-league side, Loughborough would surely start to pull clear of the drop zone. But once more, any preconceptions of easing to a first three-point haul in more than two months soon came shattering down. First Conor O'Keefe is beaten by a deft lob from Boldmere forward Joe Lyng, before the same man pops up at the far post to head home a deep free kick. Another set piece conceded.

The Mikes smelt blood and lay siege on O'Keefe's goal as they attempted to find the golden touch that would leave their opponents with nothing. Geed on by 100 eager home fans, the hosts came forward in waves but were continually repelled.

When the final whistle blows, it was light relief for the Scholars. A point would do, but with other results from around the division going against Loughborough, they find themselves only outside of the relegation places by virtue of a better goal difference than their rivals. The team are in freefall with no win in eight and they're left to turn their fortunes around without two key figures, who have gone on to pastures new.

If the negative momentum didn't stop building, a worrying spring could soon be followed by a disastrous summer.

OLYMPIC LEGACIES

It's just gone half past 11 on match day and Loughborough University Stadium is empty. Apart from one man, that is.

Tom Fletcher is surrounded by a silence that hangs across every nook and cranny of the ground, with only the slight rustle of the Lidl carrier bag he's holding providing an accompaniment to his soft footsteps. The grey-haired man slowly climbs up the stairs and pushes open the heavy door that leads into the football club's impressive conference facilities, where a hush fills the void that will be brimming with people in just three hours' time. His first port of call is the small boardroom that sits in the far corner of the long room he walks across. The view out towards the pitch to the left receives little more than a cursory glance as Tom makes a beeline for the room, places his bag on the table and starts stocking the small fridge with his horde.

It's the first of a series of well-rehearsed tasks that Tom has carried out each Saturday morning that Loughborough have been at home for the past four years. Measured, methodical and meticulous, Tom wouldn't have it any other way.

"My day starts with checking if the car will start," explains Loughborough's stoic Mr Loyalty, without even a hint of humour in his tone. "If I can't use the car, then I'd get here by bus or train. I go to Lidl to pick up some milk and cakes, and anything else we need, then I'm off down the motorway for 11ish to do the walk round.

"The stadium is a shared facility, so people don't necessarily leave it as we'd want it left. So my walk-through includes arranging the desks as we like them, checking the ice machine and that the doors and locks work properly. Coming in early gives us the chance to sort something out if it's wrong."

Walk into any non-league club in the land and you'll find a similarly dedicated clutch of volunteers who help to keep things ticking over, although when you consider the superb surroundings across the entire university, it initially surprised me that volunteers were needed at Loughborough.

Watching Tom – and the other volunteers who report for duty soon afterwards – the value they offer is huge. They are as much a key part of the club's spirit as any of the student footballers who set Loughborough apart from the norm in the first place. No job is too big or menial for the volunteers. Today, Tom's tasks range from wiping down the white tactics boards in the dressing rooms to clearing a broken bottle near the dugouts, well before the first fans begin to filter into the stadium.

A retired project manager, this is the first time Tom has been involved with a football club of any sort. In fact, when pressed to name a side that he supported, even as a youngster, he simply talks about his 'allegiance' to legendary manager Brian Clough. Living several miles north of Loughborough in an area flooded with Nottingham Forest and Derby County fans in even proportion, it's possibly no surprise that Tom found himself drawn to Old Big 'Ed and his achievements, rather than a specific club. But since answering the call for volunteers in the Loughborough area to help distribute kit to Great Britain's hopeful Olympians before London 2012, Tom has adopted the university's student side as his own. Although his link to the Leicestershire town isn't completely circumstantial.

"I came to Loughborough University in 1977 to do a master's degree in management," says Tom, taking a short break in his tasks to talk to me. Nothing is too much trouble.

"At that time, Seb Coe was here and could run like the wind. He was one of the wonders of the world back then because when he was running around the track, your brain didn't believe what your eyes were seeing. You'd think: 'nobody can run that fast' as he whizzed by. You were mesmerised and it stuck with me – I look back to my time at university and my memory is of Seb Coe running."

Coe's influence on Tom's life can't be understated. The double 1500-metre Olympic champion was instrumental in helping London be named as the host city for the 2012 Games, which is where the thirst for volunteering first awoke in Tom.

"In retirement, I wanted something to fill my time and I'm still active, so I answered an advert for volunteers for 2012," Tom adds.

"I met so many Olympic athletes and it was so gratifying to be picking kit for Tom Daly, Jessica Ennis and Mo Farah. My first picking list was for Ben Ainslie. When you saw these folks winning on TV and watched them go up on the podium, you'd see them in their kit, which was very special.

"As thank-you presents, we got an invite to the Olympic procession at The Mall in London and a few metres behind us were Coe, Princess Anne, Boris Johnson and David Cameron – it was a wonderful event. Later on, we got an invite to the royal garden party, which really was something else.

"The spirit of the Olympics was to encourage sport and a lot of the Medal Makers, as we were called, continued to volunteer at the university, helping with netball, rugby and football."

Overhearing Tom talk about how he started out at Loughborough, the ears of another volunteer prick up. After entering the room just moments before, Gordon Watson interjects: "In a way, we're examples of the lasting legacy of the Olympics. For me, volunteering will last for my entire life.

"I did my Medal Maker training in Melton Mowbray and was involved in the torch relay. That got me hooked on volunteering in sport and I found my way back into football, which has always been my passion."

Gordon and Tom have worked in perfect tandem at Loughborough for several years, although the former has been helping out for a little bit longer. While Tom was drawn by the prospect of being involved with the university, it was football that drew Gordon into a weekly pilgrimage to Loughborough. He has been involved in non-league from a young age, watching boyhood club VS Rugby at Wembley when they won the FA Vase in 1983, and becoming a regular at clubs in the capital when he moved down there for work.

Now, also a fellow retiree, Gordon shares his time between Loughborough and a part-time job at a retail store to supplement his pension.

"I rarely miss a game, and go home and away, so it's a real labour of love," he beams proudly. "I started following the university by accident. I'd moved to Loughborough for work and was looking for a non-league club to adopt. I went to Nanpantan Sports Ground, thinking Loughborough Dynamo would be at home, but they weren't. The university were playing instead while they ground-shared there and I was really impressed.

"I really liked the spirt of the university, how they prepared and the way they conducted themselves – not only on the pitch, but all the support staff off it.

"The next season, I saw an advert in the local paper to support (former performance manager) Stuart McLaren with the administration on match day, so I started helping – now this is season number seven for me."

Tom and Gordon grow busier as kick-off approaches, with first the referees and then today's opposition, Brocton, to welcome to the stadium. The mood is cheery and friendly, despite what's at stake in this afternoon's game.

Brocton, a village side from Staffordshire, looked dead certs for relegation at Christmas, having endured a nightmare first half of the season. However, following a string of impressive victories, they have clawed themselves within four points of safety – and just eight points from Loughborough.

Since they held on to take a point from Boldmere St. Michaels two weeks ago, the Scholars' form has picked up too: first beating local rivals Shepshed Dynamo 2-1, then earning a credible draw against Long Eaton United. So a strong performance at home today could re-establish a healthy cushion above the bottom three, although defeat would suck them right back into the mire.

While Gordon takes up his customary place in the announcers' box to read out the teams and keep supporters informed during the game, Tom's brief means he rarely gets to see much of the action on the pitch. As the game gets underway, with Paul Braithwaite hitting the post during an encouraging start for the hosts, Tom isn't within view of the pitch. He's back in the boardroom, clearing up after his guests and logging the takings on the gate, before starting his preparations for the half-time service.

I could never imagine spending several hours every Saturday going to a match, only to see brief snippets of it, although I'd probably have had many more enjoyable afternoons if that was the case. But that's exactly what Tom does, as he hurriedly gets everything to the required standard. It might well be the best place for a Loughborough fan at present, as the promising first few minutes soon take on an all-too-familiar twist.

When Gordon clicks the switch on the PA system to announce the first goal of the match, it's not the news he wants to deliver. Brocton are ahead, as Lee Wherton turns in from close range.

Things only get worse on 18 minutes when Jake Edwards is allowed two attempts before squeezing a shot beneath O'Keefe for 2-0. As Gordon reaches for the speaker once again, the sledgehammer of emotion he feels while watching the Scholars implode must be multiplied by the hours of selfless effort he pours into the club.

By half-time, the two-goal deficit remains. An Alex Dinsmore penalty provided brief hope after Alex Read was upended in the area, but the visitors restored their advantage within minutes after a long punt presented Nicholas Welcombe with the space to fire home.

As the whistle goes for the break, I make for the boardroom to find Tom and get his opinion on the scoreline. When I get there, he is already surrounded by cups and saucers, pouring hot drinks with his trademark friendly demeanour. There's no sign of any animosity against his team's rivals.

"Would you like a drink young man?" Tom asks me as I step closer to him. While I politely decline his offer, I'm interested in how he remains so cheery when so many football fans are more likely to spend the break bemoaning their side's frailties after such a poor first half. Instead of directly addressing Loughborough's struggles, Tom's response is measured and provides a healthy helping of perspective to football's true role in the world.

"For a number of years, I was a one-to-one carer for a relative who had age-related disabilities and progressive dementia," Tom muses.

"That's easy to say in one sentence, but when it's night after night, not knowing if you're going to be in an ambulance whizzing down to hospital, as we did on several occasions, it takes its toll. To suddenly be back in an environment with people who are nearing or at the peak of their lives is refreshing when you've been spending time with people at the end of their lives. I used to have to find that motivation from somewhere to keep that relationship going with my relative, whereas here, everybody provides motivation for you."

With Tom's poignant words ringing in my ears, it's time for the second half to begin. As I settle into my seat again, I must admit that any nervous looks at the scores around the rest of the division seem more churlish than less than half an hour ago. Maybe Tom should go down to the dressing room to do the team talk. Instead, that honour resides with Brennan and he's clearly in no mood to meekly accept defeat as he makes a double substitution: Alex Johnson and goalscorer Dinsmore being replaced by Ben Last and Jake Taylor.

It appears to have the desired effect. As Gordon squirms around in his seat, Loughborough go close to reducing the arrears with Matthew Crookes and Last both denied in quick succession by Brocton goalkeeper Aidan Stone.

Then from a corner, the ball is worked across to former Bristol City youngster Last, who steers a low effort into the net from just inside the area. Gordon cheers and joyfully announces that the score is now 3-2.

"When you do see a comeback, you feel a sense of elation and you take that into the next fixture," Gordon admits, eyes trained on the action as the Scholars go close again when Trotman flashes a drilled shot across the face of goal that evades Crookes by a matter of inches.

"I'm made to feel very involved with the team and get regular updates from management, so you really feel part of it as a volunteer. I've helped out in the dugout before and in pre-season, I even went to scout an opponent before we played them – not while we had a match of our own, of course – as we needed an extra pair of hands. In my own way, I hope I contribute a bit."

All Gordon can do today though is hope, with attention drawn to the action once more as Crookes sees another effort palmed away by Stone with an almighty swipe of the paw.

"There's another goal in this," I promise, as the electronic scoreboard counts ever closer to 90 minutes. And I'm right.

A deep cross from the right picks out Last in the area and the substitute bundles towards the ball, but somehow can't force it over the line – and Brocton break. Loughborough are caught upfield and the counter attack makes its way to Badgers forward Paul McMahon, who lifts a looping lob over the exposed O'Keefe to settle the match.

Gordon lets out a frustrated sigh, before finding the positivity to announce Brocton's fourth goal of the afternoon. It spells a damaging defeat that leaves the Scholars looking nervously over their shoulder at the drop zone, where AFC Wulfrunians sit only one win and a game in hand behind them.

While Gordon and no doubt Tom, wherever he is, remain upbeat, the sight of Brennan pulling the players together for a huddle in the centre circle highlights the severity of the danger Loughborough are facing.

"We need to stay together," Brennan can be heard rallying the despondent students that surround him. Brennan's soon joined by another little helper, as his eldest son, a toddler who spent most of the half cheering on daddy from the main stand, comes rushing to his side.

"It's a very close-knit team," says Tom, as the players begin to disperse down below. "Everyone knows everyone else and the euphoria on the team coach on the way back after an away win is incredible, although it's not quite like that when we've lost, like today.

"This is my family. I have relatives in Hong Kong, some in Shanghai and more in Cornwall. There is the odd cousin or two knocking about, but my real family are out of the area, so I have this family of players, supporters and managers instead.

"The only difference is that towards the end of the year, we know we'll lose members of our family as they graduate and go on to something new. But then we get new members coming in during the next summer."

No time to waste, Tom leaves that sentiment hanging as he heads back towards the boardroom. There are goodbyes to be said to the visitors, before another round of tidying and some more paperwork to sift through with Gordon. When Tom finally locks up the stadium gate at gone seven o'clock, it brings an end to another eight-hour shift. Win or lose, rain or shine, Tom will be back again in two weeks for the next home match.

One thing's for sure though: another defeat like this and there could be trouble on the horizon for Loughborough's happy family.

NO MORE NERVES

There are just four short miles between Shepshed and Loughborough, but the numbers at stake on the spring afternoon that the two towns' football teams clash have much bigger importance than that.

As Shepshed Dynamo's fans make the 10-minute drive down the A512's dual carriageway to Loughborough University Stadium for the penultimate match of the season, they know that a victory would go a long way to consigning their local rivals to relegation to the 10th tier of English football. And Dynamo's rowdy contingent are not in a forgiving mood.

Clumped together in a huddle to the left of Loughborough's club bar, the away supporters are clearly identifiable by the yellow team colours worn by some of their most passionate members. Shepshed may be lodged firmly in mid-table with no prospect of the dreaded drop that haunts the Scholars, but this is no dead rubber for them. They have revenge – and local pride – on their minds.

"We can help them go down today," announces one strong East Midlands accent to a fellow Dynamo fan.

"We owe them for a few weeks ago, so I don't care," comes the heartless retort of another loud voice within the posse, followed by a few snorts of laughter.

It's true. Shepshed's pride will still be stinging from the defeat just over a month ago – after all, they carry the unwanted moniker of being one of only two sides that their neighbours have beaten in the league since 3 January. And looking at the league table, they are three points that could prove valuable to Loughborough's students when the season ends in seven days' time.

Following the damaging defeat to struggling Brocton three weeks ago, the Scholars have been creeping towards safety, but in typically inconsistent fashion. A mid-week trouncing of high-flying Westfields for only their second win in 12 matches suggested that the Brocton result would be a watershed moment. Although two points from a possible nine afterwards, which included an agonising late draw with third-bottom Shawbury United, leaves them nervously looking over their shoulder again.

With just one week of the season remaining, Loughborough's Midland Premier Division status is decidedly precarious. With only this match against Shepshed and a final-day away trip to fourth-placed Lye Town to save them, the bottom of the table reads:

		Pld	Pts	GD
17	Walsall Wood	40	47	-23
18	Loughborough University	40	45	1
19	AFC Wulfrunians	39	44	-20
20	Shawbury United	40	43	-24
21	Brocton	40	34	-55
22	Tividale	40	23	-61

While their survival is still in their own hands, the remaining fixtures show why the worried looks on Loughborough fans' faces are warranted, with likely points still to come for both Shawbury and AFC Wulfrunians.

With many arriving at the ground ahead of kick-off expecting the students to lose when they travel to Lye next week, getting all three points today is crucial.

"Relegation could be a disaster," says Mat when I notice him in the main stand. "The reputation of the football programme is really important. With several other similar university teams popping up, it's more competitive than ever to get players in, so dropping down a level might make it more difficult to attract the better ones. Of course, the facilities and coaching will still be just as good, but if the better players go elsewhere, it could be difficult to stay ahead."

While Mat's pensiveness is no surprise, it is a shock to see him at all: I've just read his name on the squad list inside the bar. He's been named on the bench again with injury keeping number-two goalkeeper Jake Taylor out of the squad. But with his gloves and boots stashed at the back of the stadium announcers' box, Mat clearly doesn't expect to be called upon to swap his Loughborough polo shirt and jeans for a kit later today.

"Just watch," he says, with a smile spreading across his face. "There will be a late penalty and I'll need to come on and save the season!"

It's a rare joke among a growing tension that builds with every passing minute before kick-off. The repercussions of another defeat linger at every corner. Despite the concern that's gathering up in the main stand, a floor down and the mood is markedly different. Underneath the hustle and bustle of the arriving throng of supporters, Loughborough's players seem relaxed and are preparing for the game just like any other. The hum of idle chatter fills the dressing room as shin pads are fastened and boot laces are tightened. It's just how Brennan had planned it when he called the squad in for training yesterday evening, although it wasn't a time to fill whirring minds with a dossier of last-minute information. Instead, he handed the reins over to Ackerley, who put the players through their paces in a short session before a kick-about ensued, which included the entire squad, as well as Brennan.

Training was followed by a meal and the players stayed together to watch the live Friday evening match on TV to stop their thoughts wandering towards what is one of the club's most important fixtures since they returned to non-league football a decade ago.

Brennan had left his two-year-old son's birthday celebrations early to be with the team and although the pull of his fatherly duties was strong, he knew the importance of getting his team in the right frame of mind. Football at Loughborough is designed to be a learning curve, but this season's unexpected relegation fight is something almost all of the side has never experienced before, so Brennan's mission was to create an environment that finds the right balance between composure and passion.

Now, standing at the far end of the busy changing area with assistant Nurse by his side, Brennan looks the pillar of coolness, with his close-cut black hair and closed sunglasses hanging from the neck of his T-shirt. If he's feeling any pressure, he's not showing it, and that's the message that's conveyed to the players. As the internal door that leads to the physio's treatment table is pushed to, Brennan starts his team talk in suitably calm fashion. There's no Napoleonic speech to stir the senses and no tub-thumping war cry to heighten the blood pressure.

"At this stage, it's not down to me to impose on the lads how to do every little thing. They know by now and if they do it right, then we'll be alright today," Brennan explains, as he sends his players out for the warm-up.

"University football is quite a transient environment because a lot of these players are leaving when they graduate this summer. I've been speaking to them about being custodians of the club and although it might not be them who are here next season, they need to feel that this club is their own."

It's an incredibly salient point. With almost half of today's squad in their final year at university and preparing for pastures new in just a few months, the prospect of relegation doesn't carry the same threat as it would for players at other football clubs. Nobody is questioning that the team want to avoid their legacy becoming a relegation, but their futures aren't at stake as they would be anywhere else. Stay up or go down, the graduates will still be playing in their final home league match for Loughborough today and their next steps in life will remain the same.

Human nature, the beast that it is, dictates that it's easier to put everything on the line for something that you need rather than something that you want. It's a nagging feeling that I can't shake as I take my seat in the main stand to watch the warm-up's final throes: how will these young men react if things start to go wrong?

Whatever happens, it's clear that this is a defining moment for Loughborough. For all the talk of creating an innovative football culture that flies in the face of traditional methods, relegation would raise questions about how effective it truly is. Surely, a team backed by a university with such resource and reputation for sporting excellence should be a relative big fish at this level, not one struggling to survive.

The anxiety that's building inside me isn't evident on the pitch though. Basking in the warm spring sunshine, Loughborough's players couldn't look more at ease with the situation. There are plenty of smiles on show as the warm-up drills are completed and my optimism receives a welcome boost when, among the defensive formation that's being put through their paces, I spot the familiar figure of former captain Danny Brenan, who is answering an SOS to help Loughborough in the last couple of weeks of the season. Brenan has enjoyed a successful spell with Hednesford Town since moving to the Pitmen in November, but with a post-graduation coaching course beckoning him in the US, the centre back will be taking a hiatus from English football for the foreseeable future.

As the starting XI filter back towards the dressing room, my eyes are drawn to an unusual set piece competition that's taking place without a goalkeeper, each shot aiming into the extremities of the empty net. There are bursts of laughter as substitute Alex Johnson arrows a penalty against the inside of the post and out towards the opposite corner flag: the juxtaposition of Loughborough's perilous situation and the reality playing out in front of me continuing to collide.

Those concerns begin to evaporate once the match begins, with the Scholars taking an early stranglehold of possession. They are playing with a freedom and belief that belies their wretched run of form and inexperience as they slickly stroke the ball between them. One such move carves into the Shepshed backline, presenting an opening for Crookes, but his low left-footed effort is stopped comfortably by glovesman Laurie Pearson.

Next up, it's Brenan's turn to test Pearson, but the returning defender can only steer a volley straight at the goalkeeper after he connects with a deep free kick from the right.

With the scores still level, Shepshed's fans start to get restless, and they begin to direct frustrations at their team's struggles towards the referee.

"Which course are you taking next year, ref?" screams one loud-mouthed Dynamo fan as yet another decision goes against the visitors. Then, as if wanting to cash in on the laughter, he starts yelling at Brennan's dugout too.

"Get back in your technical area, you little shit!" yells the yellow-shirted supporter at Loughborough's manager. But just as it looks as though the derby day atmosphere is about to boil over, the abuse is policed by other members of the Shepshed crowd.

"Shut up, you'll give us a bad name," calls out a fellow fan who is standing only a few feet away from the aggressor. He's met with a disapproving grunt, but the shouts soon stop. Try using that approach at one of the world's fiercely contested derbies.

The passion in the stands appears to wake up the away side. Winger Liam Read turns inside on the right flank and unleashes a curling shot towards goal that forces O'Keefe into a diving one-handed save.

If that wasn't enough of a scare for Loughborough, there's further worrying news from elsewhere. Shawbury United, who started the day in the drop zone, have gone 1-0 up against leaders Alvechurch, leaving the Scholars only one point clear of danger as scores stand.

O'Keefe's flying save appears to shock the students back into action. First Ward-Cochrane wriggles into some space, but is stopped from pulling the trigger by a superb last-ditch challenge. Then, Bridge sees a deflected strike somehow turned round the post by Pearson, before Legg and Last also go close before the half-time whistle.

Loughborough have been the better side, but with nothing to show for their domination at the break, I start to wonder if it's going to be another day when the students don't get the result their build-up play deserves.

Elsewhere, the news is mixed. As fans anxiously scroll through scant Twitter updates on the rival clubs to find out what's happening across the region, piecemeal information reveals that Alvechurch have levelled against Shawbury and that AFC Wulfrunians are drawing 1-1 with Coventry United. Updates from the other side battling the drop, Walsall Wood, are hard to find, but there's murmurings that they're two goals down at home to Heanor Town. With Midland Football League coverage at a premium, there are plenty of eyes glued to phone screens throughout the interval as fans try to discover titbits of information from the other matches. The days of seeing football fans with transistor radios glued to their ears might be behind us but today's desperate smartphone dalliance isn't much of an upgrade.

The Loughborough players emerge for the second half knowing that Shepshed are there for the taking. And with Brennan's half-time words still ringing in their ears, the Scholars finally make a breakthrough.

Bridge's persistent running down the left gives him the chance to force a low cross into the area and Ward-Cochrane gets on the end of it to squeeze a finish beneath Pearson and into the net. A cacophony of relieved whoops and claps merge with annoyed Shepshed moans – the goal means Loughborough would be safe if scores stay the same elsewhere.

Unfortunately, that isn't the case: AFC Wulfrunians are ahead against Coventry United. Although it's academic if Loughborough seal the three points and Shawbury can't find a winner against Alvechurch.

The students are in no mood to let another team decide their fate though and continue in their search for a second goal. A ricocheted Tom Rankin effort falls perfectly for Read to be the hero, but as the teenager squares his body up to pass the ball into the net, he somehow manages to skew his shot inches wide of the far post.

Minutes later, Read provides a smart through ball to Crookes and the ginger-haired forward's effort beats Pearson and looks to be heading into the net before it smashes back off the post and hooked to safety. The knot in my stomach tells me this misfortune can't be good, although a quick scan of my phone tells me that nothing has changed in the other matches.

But then, it happens. As predictable as night follows day, the sucker punch is delivered with almost inevitable accuracy.

A seemingly innocuous throw-in is flicked on towards Shepshed's burly forward Matt Langham, who spins on the edge of Loughborough's box and places a volley across O'Keefe and into the far corner of the net. The visiting fans go berserk as the hosts slump in disappointment. It's 1-1 with less than 20 minutes remaining. The Scholars are heading for the nightmare scenario of needing a result at Lye Town on the final day.

I look up to the announcers' box where Mat and Gordon are looking dejected, while Brennan is rallying up his charges on the touchline. Now is the time for the composure he spoke of before kick-off.

Loughborough are soon back in possession and looking to calm things down before launching a final assault on Shepshed's goal. Joe Jackson plays the ball across to O'Keefe and the goalkeeper takes a loose touch on the edge of the box that alerts Langham, as the big striker launches into a sliding tackle to steal the ball. Panicked, O'Keefe tries to drag the prize away from Langham's boot, but can't get it away before the challenge makes contact and the ball squirms away. Audible gasps can be heard across the stand as O'Keefe and Langham turn to see where the ball is. Luckily, it's within the goalkeeper's reach as he hooks the clearance away upfield. Disaster averted – in Loughborough at least.

As reports of a third AFC Wulfrunians goal appear to have sealed all three points for the strugglers and no news of any kind at Shawbury, it's still looking tight at the bottom of the table.

The purples haven't given up and they launch another attack. Last pings a crossfield ball to Trotman, who jinks past his man and whips a cross into the box that picks out fellow full back Bridge, who directs a header downwards into the goal. As the net bulges, a sense of respite washes over the stadium.

The late goal is the last noteworthy action of the match, but as the final whistle sounds on Loughborough's success, there isn't time to celebrate yet. There's still no news from Shawbury, with no updates on the match for almost half an hour.

"Any news?" Brennan shouts up to the congregation of fans gathered in the stand. There's no definitive reply.

Muted congratulations spread among the players. The uncertainty reminds me of the now-famous pictures of Manchester United's players hanging on for news that rivals Manchester City had scored two injury-time goals to nick the 2012 Premier League. But this time, I'm hoping for no such drama.

As Brennan waits by the touchline nearest to the stand, the players form a huddle on the opposite side of the pitch. Then they cheer and the scramble for updates begins again in the stand.

"They must have a phone in there," says one fan. "That's it, Shawbury have drawn – we're safe," another affirms.

Brennan looks up again for confirmation and waits for the thumbs up before greeting his players with warm hugs and fist pumps. They've saved Loughborough's season. In the box, Mat pulls up a screen that shows how the league table will look tonight. It makes more palatable reading.

		Pld	Pts	GD
17	Loughborough University	41	48	2
18	AFC Wulfrunians	40	47	-17
19	Walsall Wood	41	47	-25
20	Shawbury United	41	44	-24
21	Brocton	41	34	-60
22	Tividale	41	24	-61

"It was absolutely awful down there waiting for the other results," Brennan admits when I see him in the bar after the celebrations have died down.

"I know these teams and the league well enough that I didn't expect Shawbury to lose, but our destiny was in our own hands and I'm glad we did our bit.

"The lads just love playing football, which is probably the biggest problem we have because sometimes there has to be an emphasis on results on a day like today. Sometimes, you have to sacrifice what you want to do out there to win the game, and we did that.

"There has been no pressure on my job despite the bad run we've been on and we tried not to pass that on to the players, which makes this quite a unique place to be."

It's a testimony that I've been hearing all season long and although the league campaign is coming to an end, there's still time for Loughborough to show quite how special it is.

GERRARD WATCH

"When's Steven Gerrard getting here?" asks a young fan to nobody in particular.

Dressed head to toe in a red Liverpool kit, the boy looks longingly towards the gap in the hedge that leads to the car park, willing for his hero to appear. The question hangs unanswered for a few seconds before another member of the small group of children huddled next to Loughborough University's beach volleyball court musters a reply.

"Steven Gerrard will be here in two minutes," he says, with all the conviction of an eight-year-old who has just told the perfect white lie to impress his friends. For a little while, at least. An audible rumble of excitement can be heard among the bunch of young friends as they prepare themselves for their idol's arrival.

The youngsters are not the only ones hoping to meet the former England and Liverpool captain at Loughborough University Stadium tonight. Swarms of students and football fans from across the town populate the pathway that winds past the Holywell training pitches and across the small footbridge to the turnstiles.

It's the busiest I've ever seen the ground for a match and as I show my ticket to gain entry to the heavily stewarded grandstand, I pass a plethora of photographers and cameramen who are here to capture the occasion. After all, it's not every day that Liverpool are in town.

The Scholars may only have secured their status in the ninth tier of the English game 10 days ago, but it hasn't stopped them bringing down the curtain on the 2016/17 season by hosting one of the world's most famous football clubs. With the little matter of qualification to next year's Champions League still to play for in the Premier League, the Reds haven't sent a full-strength side to take on the students though. Instead, it's their academy team that are warming up in front of a rapidly growing crowd, who are undeterred by the news that no Liverpool first teamers will be on show.

The marquee match was announced a few weeks ago and coincided with rumours that Gerrard was set to take over Liverpool's under-18s in the summer. And when that news was confirmed in the past seven days, the fervour started to build about the prospect of his appearance on a watching brief from the stands. Cue plenty of eager glances towards the row of 10 empty seats with printed 'Liverpool FC' signs taped to them.

While most of the ground are on Gerrard watch, the next generation of Reds stars are being put through their paces on the field. Surrounded by a large academy coaching team, with the famous liver bird emblem embroidered on their shirts, the team look energetic and technically gifted as they take part in a series of short drills.

On the other half of the pitch, Loughborough are being prepared for their big night by interim performance manager Ackerley, who was given the nod to lead proceedings from the dugout as a university fixture rather than a non-league duty.

"We've been preparing for this match since the Shepshed result that secured our safety," says Ackerley a few minutes later, as we pass each other in the tunnel that leads to the pitch.

"Training has been going well and we've watched a video of how

Chelsea played against them in an under-18s match last week, so we're going to set up in a similar way. Now all we've got to do is be as good as Chelsea – it's that easy!" he remarks with a big grin on his face, realising the irony.

If Loughborough are going to cause an upset, they'll certainly have something to remember the occasion by. As yet another camera barges past me to get some pitchside footage for Loughborough Students' Union Media's TV broadcast, I look up to the stand, where three temporary gantries have been created to film the match. The small room normally left for Tom and Gordon's pre-match hosting has also been cleared and replaced by a nerve centre of video feeds and student producers, who will orchestrate the coverage.

Despite all the furore, this isn't the first time Loughborough have hosted one of the country's big boys at the stadium. Since moving in to their home in 2012, the student side has faced Manchester United, Tottenham Hotspur and Leicester City, and gone up against future internationals, including Marcus Rashford.

It's part of the university's unique allure that they're able to attract such illustrious opposition to play them. Prior to re-entering the non-league ranks a decade ago, it was these friendly matches against the youth teams of the country's professional clubs that set Loughborough's football programme apart from any other. Over the decades, frequent visits from top Midlands sides, such as Notts County, West Brom and Aston Villa, became commonplace as an array of student XIs pitted their wits against players who were hoping to graduate into the Football League in the future. For the initiated, there were plenty of stars on show back then.

"The university played at a ground on Browns Lane at the time and would play against these teams with professional players in them," recalls

Loughborough local John Pearman, who greets me in the main stand.

"The friendly matches would be on a Wednesday afternoon and there was a grass bank by the side of the pitch so that spectators could go and watch. At the time, a lot of the managers of the local teams used to go down to the university on a Wednesday to see who was playing because the standard was so high.

"Loughborough used to have some good players back then and would do well. I used to manage a local team, so I'd come down and once tried to sign a guy I thought looked good. I said to him 'come to play for us and we'll give you a couple or three beers'. It turned out to be Lawrie Sanchez, who was playing professionally for Reading at the time!"

John has been watching Loughborough's university side since the days of Bob Wilson and co in the 60s, and has an extra-special reason to be interested tonight. Despite the spring-like weather today, John is dressed in a red, woolly hat with the words 'Red All Over The Land' emblazoned on it: the name of the Liverpool fanzine he's editor for.

"I'm supporting both teams," he says. "It means that whatever the result tonight, I can't go home disappointed. It's great to see them playing each other."

As one of the Loughborough University supporters with the longest affinity with the club, John's almost-encyclopaedic memory of times gone by is vivid. Just talking to him about matches from the past is like opening a tomb of seemingly forgotten tales – most of which are laced with glory. With the crowd burgeoning around us, it might be a novelty for me to see hundreds of people turning up to see Loughborough play, but for John it's not even on the same scale as some of the matches he's been to in the past.

"When Loughborough drew Hitchin in the quarter-finals of the FA Amateur Cup in 1961, it was estimated that 10,000 people came to watch the match," John harks back to the glorious run by what many would say was Loughborough's greatest-ever team.

"The town really came together for that cup run. Back then, Saturday afternoons were all about football, although there's so many other things to do now. You could have a local cup final between two pub teams and you'd get more than 1,000 people watching it back in the 60s and 70s.

"When Loughborough beat Bishop Auckland in the second round [of the Amateur Cup] in 1961, the result made BBC News at night because Bishop Auckland were the Manchester United – or Liverpool – of amateur football back then. When Bishop Auckland played in Amateur Cup finals at Wembley, there could be 80,000 people turning up to watch them, so there were five or six thousand there for the Loughborough match."

Tonight's attendance is expected to challenge the 1,000 mark, with throngs of people turning up outside, hoping to get in. Down behind one of the goals, a clutch of students dressed as hot dogs, as well as a solitary ketchup bottle for good measure, are adding extra colour to proceedings.

With only 10 minutes to go before kick-off, there's still no sign of Gerrard. The party of Liverpool representatives settle down in their seats at the top of the stand, with plenty of eyes scanning across their faces to see if the man himself is making an appearance. While it doesn't look like the famous number eight is going to join them, his new boss has taken a seat. Liverpool Academy Director Alex Inglethorpe may not be a household name, but it's under his stewardship that the stars of tomorrow are being cultivated. The former Exeter City boss has been heading up youth development at Liverpool's Melwood training ground since August 2014, and despite the relative difference in profile between the Reds and Loughborough, he believes his players will learn valuable lessons from their university visit.

"This is a really good challenge for the young players," Inglethorpe tells me. "I've been to Loughborough before with teams, so I know exactly what level it is here – and it gives our players the chance to see what elite looks like in terms of facilities and the students. It's a very good environment to show our younger players what it's like and what can be achieved if they take the educational route."

While the most-talented teenagers, such as Ben Woodburn and Trent Alexander-Arnold, are already making an impact on the first team at Anfield, the sad reality is that most of the youngsters currently in the academy won't make it big. So tonight's match, which has followed on from a day spent hearing from Loughborough students and touring the campus, is about more than just 90 minutes of football: it's a glimpse into the crystal ball at a possible future. But convincing academy dropouts from the big clubs to consider university as a back-up option isn't so easy. The drop from the glitz and glamour of a state-of-the-art academy is particularly rough and the harsh realities of the shattered dreams that the rejects face will be devastating. Although Inglethorpe believes this is a responsibility that falls on the clubs themselves to help with.

"As clubs and an industry, we're getting better at looking at the boys who don't make it because football is such a tough industry to break into," he says. "But not everybody is going to be lucky enough to come to a university like this: you have to be academically capable, as well as physically capable. Those boys who are, we'd definitely push towards having qualifications if football didn't work out.

"Whether university can be a route back into [professional] football is harder though. The number of people who go to university and end up with a new career are few and far between, but anything is possible. I'm sure clubs do look at university football because there's plenty of potential there if someone is talented enough and they want to trade their education for a football career. But that's not for everybody – playing part-time and carrying on with your studies might be the most sensible option."

As the players emerge from the tunnel at the bottom right-hand corner of the pitch, the assembled crowd sound their appreciation. The dazzling scoreboard on the far side confirms the occasion, as it reads Loughborough 0 Liverpool 0. It's time to show that attending a professional academy isn't the only route to success on the football pitch.

For once, the Scholars aren't the youngsters of the piece, as Liverpool line up with several 15- and 16-year-olds in their ranks. The additional respect that the trademark Liverpool red grants the visitors, paired with the incredible physiques that British academies cherish, means it's hard to tell the age difference. The home fans certainly don't care and are baying for the students to strike an early blow when a through ball towards Ward-Cochrane draws an excitable roar within moments of kick-off, but the fast reactions of Liverpool number one Caoimhin Kelleher see to the danger as the Irishman gets there in the nick of time.

The game soon settles into a rhythm, but not one that many of the regulars have been familiar with this season. The blood-and-thunder high tempo that oozed from every pore of the non-league matches hosted at this stadium is forgotten as the two teams take it in turns to play keep-ball across the backline.

Liverpool, marshalled supremely by midfielder Liam Coyle, who with an easy posture and perfectly tucked-in shirt has the demeanour of a chiselled veteran rather than a young 17-year-old, look the more dangerous. And when the rapid Liam Miller escapes down the left flank, it's only the smothering arms of Conor O'Keefe that stop him from burning off the entire Loughborough right wing.

The experience of playing regularly in senior football, albeit the Midland Football League, begins to show as the purples start to put themselves about. A series of hard challenges by captain Legg and another from Poxon stir the locals.

Then breaking down the right, Trotman shows that it's not all hard work and industry in Loughborough's ranks. The full back, whose spell in the Football League with Luton Town might have ended differently if it wasn't for injury, takes control of a bouncing ball and hits a dipping half volley past Kelleher and into the net. Cue mass celebration.

The locals can scarcely believe their eyes as the scoreboard clicks over to show that the hosts are ahead against the five-time European champions.

The Reds won't lie down and continue to probe in the final third, but time and again Loughborough get something on the ball to break up the attacks. Then the blonde-haired Lewis Longstaff escapes down the right and fires a low cross into the penalty area, evading everyone but Miller, who takes one touch before pulling back to equalise. Only the ball doesn't go in, as Trotman and O'Keefe somehow get in the way to clear the danger.

As the whistle goes for half-time at 1-0 to Loughborough, the smiles all around the stadium tell their own story. While I negotiate my way through the hordes of people heading inside for a half-time drink, I spot someone who might not be so happy with what he's seeing.

Christoph Ivanusch probably hoped to be out on the pitch playing for Loughborough tonight, but the diehard Liverpool fan has had to settle for a seat in the stands instead. It's been a few months since I've seen the Austrian exchange student, as his early season ambitions have dissipated following a difficult campaign. But despite his disappointment at not making the squad, he's still as cheery as ever.

"I want Loughborough to win tonight," he admits. "Of course, I'm a

Liverpool fan but I know the Loughborough lads and have been training with them for the match, so I've got to want them to get the win.

"I hoped that I'd be in the squad tonight, but I didn't do well enough in training. It's disappointing, but we have a lot of good players out there."

It's been the story of Ivanusch's season. After studiously watching the Scholars' matches until he received international clearance to play in September, the centre back got his chance to turn out for the first team in a handful of matches, but struggled to hold down a regular place in the squad. It meant that, initially, he was consigned to more afternoons watching matches from the stands and soon after, it wasn't unusual not to see him at all.

There had been talk of Ivanusch making tonight's squad, due to his affinity to Liverpool, although a red card in Saturday's league match against Lye Town may well have put an end to any sentiment.

"It happens sometimes as a defender," he brushes off. "I think I've done alright when I've had the chance this year, but that's football and sometimes it doesn't work out.

"While things haven't gone exactly how I'd hoped this season, it's still been a great experience. I've learned a lot training with the squad and when I went home at Easter, I played with my old team and noticed how much I've learned by playing in England. I'm not sure if I'll rejoin them when I move back to Austria in the summer, but I'll definitely find a team to play for."

With Ivanusch completing his year's placement at Loughborough and several of the players appearing in their final match for the university, an end-of-term feel hangs over the evening. As the players emerge for the second half, they could be giving themselves the perfect send-off.

The match soon settles into a similar rhythm to the first half, with Liverpool dominating possession but failing to create many clear-cut chances, bar a Rafael Camacho strike that flashes wide of O'Keefe's far post.

Given more time to play, Loughborough are enjoying the chance to show what they can do with the ball. Another neat interchange on the edge of the area sets Ward-Cochrane through and the striker pulls back a low centre into Crookes' path, where the student pulls off an audacious flick with his hind leg to turn the ball into the goal.

"Ohhhhh, what a goal!" purrs a Loughborough fan as the crowd jump up in united celebration. "Who's the Premier League side?" shouts another.

Down on the pitch, the players are huddled together in jubilation, while the exuberant Ackerley beats the air in joy. The struggling non-leaguers – a team made up of university students and Football League rejects – are on their way to a famous win.

First they need to dig in to protect their lead, as Liverpool flood forward in search of a goal. Substitute Herbie Kane narrowly misses from close range and O'Keefe turns round another effort that's whistling towards the bottom corner.

The clock on the scoreboard continues to count down towards the final whistle. Not long to go. Liverpool shot, saved. Defenders throw themselves in the way to block a further chance. Then comes the final whistle. It's over. Loughborough University have beaten Liverpool.

A surge of noise erupts around the stadium as the players embrace. The cameras fill the pitch again to record the university's glory and Ackerley is grabbed by a man with a microphone to do an interview for Liverpool FC TV. "We haven't scored one goal like that all season, let alone two," he says to the camera. "It's been a great experience."

Ackerley isn't the only man glowing after the match; so is his opposite number Neil Critchley. The departing under-18s boss, who is stepping up to take over the Reds' under-23s when Gerrard starts his new role in the summer, has never had the privilege of visiting Loughborough before and has been blown away by what he's seen.

A midfielder of little reputation in his playing days, Critchley knows a thing or two about what it's like to be a footballer whose dreams don't come true, after bouncing around non-league with Leigh Genesis and Hyde United, following his release from Crewe Alexandra as a youngster. The 38-year-old eventually found a career in coaching and knows how important it is to find a good base to bounce back again.

"When you turn up and walk around campus, you're like 'wow, this is elite'," Critchley gushes. "When we came in on the bus, you see the athletics stadium, then there's someone playing cricket, then you look over to see the 3G astroturf, and the swimming pool. Everywhere you look, it's immaculate – our boys were really taken aback by it.

"I was fortunate enough to come from Crewe and their facilities are outstanding for League Two, but I've been to other clubs lower down and Loughborough blow their socks off. This is better than a lot of Football League clubs and provides something different.

"The fact is that not everybody is going to make it in football. Hopefully, they will at Liverpool, if not somewhere else professionally but if not, this is a viable option. I wouldn't mind working or playing here every day, it's an unbelievable place."

For all his positivity, Critchley reveals that the biggest hurdle that universities like Loughborough face to become a widely considered route into the pro game is perception, with culture dictating that players see a move to education as a resignation that their dream of making it will never come true.

"Because of how many levels we've got in England and the number of professional clubs there are, the boys see playing in the Conference or League Two as a way to retain their hope that they'll be able to get back to the top. But they don't see university as a chance to do that," he adds in a steady Mancunian accent.

"One of the Loughborough boys we spoke to earlier today said that when he came here, he felt as though he was failing a bit. But speaking now, he's delighted with the decision he's made and he's still hopeful of getting back into pro football. It can happen.

"The staff are asking, if you don't make it at Liverpool, would an option like coming here be better than going to a lower league club, where the facilities aren't as good and you're not being paid a significant amount of money? You come out of here with an education, so you might be better off three, four, five years down the line than if you stay in football trying to fight for a professional career. Whether our boys see that though, I'm not sure, but we want to start changing their thinking a bit. If today affects one person, then it's worth it."

By the time I head back up to the bar after chatting with Critchley, the ground is almost empty, with students and fans excitedly chattering about what they've just seen. But there's one rumour that just won't let up, despite the result.

"Was Gerrard here in the end, then?" asks one of the Loughborough coaching team.

"Oh, yeah," replies Mat with a cheeky grin. "He was sat at the back of the stand in a hoody so nobody could tell it was him. He was here all game."

The football coordinator's bombshell brings a few disbelieving sniggers. Until the myth starts to grow legs once again. "The trouble is," says the coach, "after all that has happened today, Mat could be telling the truth."

TRACK TO THE FUTURE

James Ellis stands on the side of the pitch with his arms folded across his chest, partially covering his Great Britain polo shirt.

Watching from his technical area, Ellis's gaze is firmly fixed on the Kazan Arena pitch in front of him. His steely focus unwavering, despite the 10,000 increasingly irate Russians surrounding him. The louder their frustration gets, the greater the intense feeling of pride inside Ellis grows.

It's 2013 and Ellis's Great Britain Universities' football team are in the Russian city of Kazan for the semi-final of the World University Games. The host's side is heaving with experienced pros, including a full international and several names who have appeared in the Champions League, but they're struggling to break down 10-man Britain's resilient defence. Circling like hungry wolves, the Russians huff and puff as they try to blow the plucky Brits' house down with a second goal. It must only be a matter of time. Yet, in less than an hour, Head Coach Ellis and his patchwork of students picked from non-league outposts across the UK will be celebrating winning a place in the final, after grabbing a late equaliser and triumphing on penalties.

Despite defeat to France in the showcase match a few days later, it's an experience none of Great Britain's underdogs will ever forget. Their silver medal achievement is even more impressive when you consider that Russia aren't the only nation that have taken a squad punctuated with professionals to the student games.

While plenty of water has passed under the bridge in the four years since that glorious night in south-west Russia, the tale of how an unfancied collection of British footballers showed the world what they are capable of is a marker for the potential buried away in the country's education ranks. It should shine brightly as a beacon of hope for the sector's university clubs, but instead it's one of a few standalone stories that offer no more than a shard of light at what could be achieved in a different world.

When I chat to Ellis, I expect him to talk passionately about a future where university football becomes a more respected route to the professional game as it continues to chip away at the more traditional establishment. Although the reality, it seems, is quite different.

"Maybe I'm being cynical, but I can't ever see the university sector playing a role in the pyramid," he says as we chat on a wet Tuesday afternoon.

"It's a tricky one because I don't think the football industry sees a place for education-based football programmes contributing to a pathway. Programmes running out of further-education colleges or universities are always going to be there for the savvier family – parents, sons and daughters – who come out of the game and need a second avenue. But the Premier League is never going to say, let's try running an academy set-up out of a university. I just can't see it happening – it's seen as a grassroots, alternative route."

For a man who spent 13 years playing and working in a variety of positions at Loughborough, and has since gone on to work wonders with Great Britain Universities and BUCS, it's a damning indictment.

Ellis now spends most of his time travelling across Europe scouting players for Championship side Fulham and Swedish Allsvenskan club Ostersunds, but still maintains a vested interest in higher-education football as founder of sports transition organisation Switch The Play. For all the impact he can see university football having on individuals though, Ellis thinks a wider cultural shift needs to happen at the FA before it can ever become recognised.

"Players may come through the system and develop late, or develop a resilience to go back into pro football and say 'I'm going to show you' – there are enough examples of that to ring true," he continues.

"Being highly controversial, in the time I ran the programme, we never found any support from the powers that be, from the national governing body, to say this is a good idea. There's a glass ceiling, so while Loughborough are in the pyramid, they can't go any further because of their status.

"The FA has made a clear line in the sand constitutionally that university sides can't go past Step Five because the FA doesn't think a public service should be able to play in the football pyramid, which when you look at it is ridiculous. There are clubs going out of business left, right and centre by being poorly run, but I don't see many universities going out of business."

The rule was introduced in 2009 after Team Bath climbed into the Conference South and continued their march towards their ambition of becoming the first student side to reach the Football League. Rather than it being a case of flying too close to the sun, the club fell foul of Football Conference rules about the constitution of its clubs and duly withdrew its membership.

Despite the rule capping the progress of university sides in England, the same doesn't exist elsewhere in the British Isles. When I visited Shelley Kerr at Stirling University earlier in the season, she told me that she didn't know of any reason why her side couldn't go up into the Scottish Football League if they were to win the Lowland League and subsequent promotion play-off.

And in Wales, Loughborough's BUCS conquerors Cardiff Met nearly went one step further after they came within one match of earning a Europa League qualification berth after finishing strongly in the Welsh Premier Division. A 1-0 defeat to Bangor City in the European play-off meant that the Archers missed out on the chance to become the first student team to play in continental competition. It is another example of what can be achieved.

"There are pockets of good work going on," Ellis explains. "Stirling are doing their bit in Scotland and if you look at what Cardiff Met have achieved in the Welsh Prem too, but it's more difficult in England.

"In theory, Loughborough could set themselves up as a limited company, call themselves Loughborough Football and run a club, but that goes against the organisation for universities, so clubs are not set up correctly in ordinance with football governance.

"Universities do still see the benefit though: when I was at Loughborough, we saw it as wanting to play competitive football and BUCS was never enough. Our better players would go off all around the country at the weekend to play for other sides and we were missing a trick. It's about developing the person as a player, and we're better off keeping them altogether so the better ones have the chance to get better because they're in this environment.

"There is a place for university football clubs so that more kids can play organised football in a positive environment. It's those institutions that are ambitious enough to say it's a priority for us to push men's and women's football in pyramid, and I don't see why, when there are 10 steps of non-league, that these places shouldn't be encouraged to do so."

Despite the restrictions on the growth of English university teams, there's no doubting the positive impact they have on clubs further up the pyramid. Apart from the players who have moved on up the leagues after holing up in education, the array of former uni players and students making their voice heard is huge – especially from Loughborough.

With a host of former students taking on senior roles at the FA and at some of the top clubs in the land, the 'forgotten majority', as Ellis calls them, are showing what an impact they can have given the right opportunity. And it's there that Ellis thinks that university football can help people who have had setbacks, as it allows them to regroup, learn new skills and stay in the industry they've always craved to be in. That's where the ethos behind Switch The Play comes in again.

"It's set up to help those people who are in a situation where they've got to make a decision," Ellis tells me. "It could be the 16-year-old who is being released and needs help and advice on what to do because the bottom has fallen out of their world. It's for those guys and girls who are coming to the end of their playing career and have no plans for retirement, and then there's those who have gone on to be managers or coaches already.

"I've talked about Loughborough having a Switch The Play development programme that can run a team that's holistic, so it's not just about producing players. It's feeding the system with good coaches, and high-quality sports scientists and analysts, so there is another route for players by continuing their education and learning another skill.

"An example of how this could work is a lad I've heard about in the Football League, who is on £2,000 a week. He's not good enough for his club's league and has been sent on loan but hasn't done very well there either. His academy don't want to lose him because someone else might sign him, so they want to give him £4,000 a week. So in three years' time when he gets released and can't get a new club and goes somewhere else to earn £500 a week where he struggles, the club will have let that lad down. Those sort of lads needs a safety net and that could be housed at an institution like Loughborough.

"What I don't believe is that everyone on that programme should be studying for a degree because not everybody can. You can make a collaborative link with a vocational provider at Loughborough College or an apprenticeship, and you still give them that thing they've been living for all of their life, which is football."

While that sort of approach may still be several years away, the examples highlighting the possible benefits of using higher education as a springboard are plain to see. Names like Bradley Pritchard and Robbie Simpson stack up to show the number of players who have bounced back into the professional game with that sort of support, while Stirling University's support of Kerr as Britain's only female coach of a men's team speaks for itself.

Since I met Kerr on that February day in East Kilbride, she has scored herself a new role as Scotland Women's national coach. That means she's stepping back out of the men's game and leaves as a much more well-rounded individual, making no secret of her ambition to return to the male sport again in the future.

Then there's Paul Tisdale, who has used his experience as manager at Team Bath to achieve the improbable in modern-day football and spend 11 years at the helm of Exeter City in League, which makes him the second-longest-serving manager in the top four leagues.

Another man to do things differently is Graham Potter, a one-capped England under-21 international who turned to university after retiring to do a sports science degree. It opened the door for him to get football roles at Hull University and Leeds Metropolitan, before he took the manager's job at Ostersunds in Sweden, where he has led them to three promotions and a Swedish Cup win using a holistic approach.

The question is: how much of their success is down to the university experience or is it a certain type of person whose natural development included a pit stop in education?

"It's like everything in life," answers Ellis. "Going through university and everything it brings gives you a broad sense of some really amazing touch points of the life in front of you. It's a completely changed environment to be in and is a lot different to what you'd do at school or at a football club. I don't think it's for everyone, but people who go through it do get a taste for a different aspect of their life – it makes you curious and it made me curious.

"What is for everyone is making the best of yourself. Having some ambition doesn't equal doing a rocket science degree, but it is more than doing the everyday norm if you've got it in you. And let's be honest, if ou haven't, you're probably not going to make it as a professional footballer anyway. People like Graham and Paul [Potter and Tisdale] are very good examples of that."

So with enough role models to show the football industry what can be achieved in football programmes like Loughborough's, perhaps there's hope that the winds of change might alter perceptions of university football programmes after all.

I've got one last burning issue that I'd like to discuss with Ellis. While he's been cautious in his optimism about what has been achieved in the past, I can't stop thinking that if all of the great people can be unified, then a university programme could work. I've certainly seen enough of Loughborough in their facilities and personnel to suggest they could offer a more-than-credible alternative to the status quo. So I ask Ellis to step into a world where university clubs could move up the pyramid freely and tell me what he thinks they could accomplish then.

"It's a great question," he replies thoughtfully, taking a few seconds to consider his answer. "When I was at Loughborough, I always said that with the way we set up the programme – with degree students only, not getting paid a penny and letting any players go if they're good enough to play higher – we could make the Southern Premier League (the seventh tier). Then if we started to add in a couple of external players that might add real value to the programme and coach lower down the club or set up a community programme, there's an opportunity to get in and around the Conference.

"The other idea is having regional collaborations. So you'd have Loughborough University fronting up the brand, but you'd have a relationship with, say, Oxford University and Nottingham Trent, and their better two or three players would be considered for a professional non-league programme.

"Could you get a team in the Football League? I think you'd have to invest in it. I'm not sure the future is a university football club playing in the league though – I'd love it to happen and I've been trying to make it happen for years, but I can't see a dent in the wall at the moment."

If that day ever arrives, you can bet that Ellis won't be far away. But this time, he won't be the only one watching with intent.

ROLL OF HONOUR

KEITH BLUNT
A coach held in huge regard by his peers, Blunt managed at Sutton United before taking posts at Malmo and Viking in Scandinavia. After moving back to Britain in 1987, Blunt was a youth-team coach at Tottenham Hotspur and head coach of the FA's famous Centre of Excellence at Lilleshall. After the FA's national school closed its doors in 1999, Blunt headed to China as he attempted to grow the sport in the world's most-populated nation. Blunt sadly died in August 2016, aged 77.

KEN BOWRON
The name Ken Bowron is synonymous with scoring goals north of the border. The Loughborough graduate netted a record 50 goals for Berwick Rangers in the 1960s and is one of the Gers most prolific goalscorers.

Bowron wasn't always destined to be a goalscorer though and used to keep net as a youngster, before showing his striking prowess in a junior game for Newcastle United when they were short of an attacker. After bagging four goals and the match ball, Bowron never looked back. Although he did turn down the chance to sign a pro contract at the Magpies to go to Loughborough instead – a move which paved the way for his Berwick heroics.

ALAN BRADSHAW
Bradshaw's professional playing career started at Blackburn Rovers back in 1962, but it's not in Lancashire that he made his name. The midfielder left Ewood Park to join Crewe Alexandra after three years and a handful of appearances.

And it was at the Alex that Bradshaw became a hero, as he racked up nearly 300 league appearances – not to mention 50 league goals. He spent almost a decade playing for Crewe, with one of his proudest moments coming when he helped them earn promotion from the Fourth Division in 1967-68.

ANDY CALE

One of British football's most decorated managers in recent years, Cale won five successive Welsh Premier League titles spanning three spells as boss at The New Saints (formerly Total Network Solutions). While at TNS, Cale led the club to its first Champions League campaign – losing 6-2 on aggregate to Levadia Tallinn from Estonia in the first qualifying round.

While Cale is best known for his work in Welsh football, he has been working behind the scenes at the FA for more than 17 years and is currently head of player development and research.

TOM CURTIS

Curtis put the 'lazy student' tag to shame when he was at Loughborough: combining his degree with turning out for both the university football team and pro club Chesterfield. The midfielder played a key role in the Spireites' unlikely run to the FA Cup semi-final in 1997 during a seven-year stay at the Derbyshire club.

Now an FA youth coach developer, Curtis cut his teeth in the coaching world when he returned to Loughborough to end his playing career and even took the reins as Antigua & Barbuda's national team boss before moving back to the UK. Curtis was one of the management team who instigated Loughborough's return to non-league in 2007.

CHRIS DAVIES

The former Welsh youth international could become a big name in the British game over the next few years as he continues his rise up the ranks.

A sports science graduate in 2007, Davies went on to work at a host of top clubs, including Reading, Liverpool and Swansea City under Brendan Rodgers. Now the assistant manager at Rodgers' latest post – with Scottish champions Celtic – 32-year-old Davies is experiencing the ups and downs of the game alongside one of the country's most promising managers.

JAMES ELLIS

James Ellis breathes university football and has been involved since he enrolled at Loughborough to do a geography degree in 1996. After opting to do a masters, Ellis was the Athletic Union president before getting his first break into non-league as manager of Loughborough Dynamo.

It didn't spell the end of Ellis's involvement in university sport and after taking several roles alongside his job at Dynamo, he became Loughborough's director of football. Ellis was part of the team that helped the Scholars re-enter non-league football and was head coach of Great Britain Universities' men's football team for seven years – leading the side to unlikely appearances in the 2011 and 2013 finals.

Since leaving full-time university employment, Ellis is a senior scout at Championship side Fulham and a director for Switch The Play, a social enterprise that helps people to fulfil their potential through sport.

SAM ERITH

A current member of England's national team set-up, Erith was kept on when Gareth Southgate was named national team boss after being appointed by Roy Hodgson. Erith combines his role as England's performance coach with a full-time position at Manchester City, where he is head of performance.

Erith doesn't just look after goings-on at the Etihad though, he also oversees sports science and medicine at New York City and Melbourne City, which are also owned by the Citizens' benefactors. Erith is another of Loughborough's Premier League champions after City won the 2014 Premier League title.

GREG FEE

There aren't many footballers who can claim to have a degree in maths. But that's not all Fee has to show for his time at Loughborough – it provided him with a springboard to tot up a playing career that spanned almost two decades.

The centre back's first move was to Bradford City in 1982, but after leaving Valley Parade two years later, he took a whistle-stop tour up and down the divisions: counting Sheffield Wednesday, Preston North End and Mansfield Town among his list of former clubs.

MATT REEVES

One of Loughborough's most unlikely champions, Reeves was on the staff at Leicester City as the Foxes stunned the world by winning the Premier League title in 2015-16. The head of fitness and coaching at Leicester is in his second spell at the King Power Stadium after he followed former boss Nigel Pearson to Hull City earlier in 2011.

Dreams of winning championships and Champions League nights were distant back when Reeves was studying sports science and playing at full back in the BUCS leagues for Loughborough.

DARIO GRADI

The long-serving Crewe Alexandra boss achieved legendary status at Gresty Road during an incredible 24-year tenure at the helm between 1983 and 2007 – returning for another two years in the hot seat in 2009.

Crewe were famous for nurturing a series of talented youngsters during Gradi's time at the club, something that might have been influenced by his teacher training at Loughborough. The course helped Gradi get his first teaching job at Glyn Grammar School in Epsom, before he embarked on a career in football.

DAN HARRIS

While Harris might not have made it big in the game as a player, he has certainly made an impact as a coach. In a fiercely competitive market that sees managers and coaches hired and fired at will, Harris has carved out a 15-year career as a coach – and it shows no sign of coming to an end.

While studying a degree in PE and sports science at Loughborough, Harris played and coached the football side. From there, he worked with the youth team at Peterborough United before getting his first big break as a sports scientist at Coventry City in 2002.

Harris went on to play key roles at Birmingham City, West Brom and Celtic, while also helping with England's youth teams, and chose a change of direction in 2014 to become assistant head coach at South Korean K League side, Seoul E-Land.

RICHARD HAWKINS

Now at Manchester United, sports scientist Hawkins is a name that is revered by his fellow students. After working up the ranks at the FA, West Brom and Sheffield United, Hawkins was appointed head of human resources at Old Trafford in 2008 and has been there ever since. Hawkins was brought in to not only work with the household names that pull on United's famous red shirt but to shape the club's entire human performance structure. No pressure, then.

BARRY HINES

OK, so Hines was an author. But he also turned out in a stellar Loughborough University team before penning his most famous masterpiece, A Kestrel for a Knave, which was adapted into cult film Kes.

Hines played as a right back in a side that included future Arsenal and Scotland goalkeeper Bob Wilson, and is understood not to have been interested in reading books until one of his former teammates chucked him a copy of Animal Farm. The rest, as they say, is history.

LEE HOWARTH

A defender with more than 400 senior appearances, Howarth's ascent to the Football League started back in the early 90s, when his performances for the Scholars saw him captain Great Britain at the World University Games in 1991.

Howarth went on to play for Peterborough United, Mansfield Town and Barnet throughout a 12-year career that followed.

MARK HULSE

One of Loughborough's secret network of graduates that have infiltrated the British game. Hulse played for the Scholars during his time at university and is now one of Jose Mourinho's fitness coaches at Manchester United. His stint at Old Trafford comes on the back of working in similar roles at Crystal Palace, Newcastle United and Liverpool.

CHARLES HUGHES

Charles Hughes's middle initials are FC – and it wouldn't be a surprise if they stood for Football Club. While Hughes was criticised for his old-school approach to tactics later in his career, his record as coach of England's amateur and Great Britain's Olympic teams can't be sniffed at (winning 48 out of 77 matches), before joining the FA's back room.

Hughes is perhaps most famous for his statistical analysis and his belief that getting the ball forward as quickly as possible was the most effective way of scoring, with goals typically scored from moves consisting of three passes or fewer. And where did it all begin? With a PE qualification from Loughborough.

CHRIS JONES

A serial collector of Premier League winners' medals, Jones has worked under several super managers in his 11 years at Chelsea. Promoted to the first team shortly before Carlo Ancelotti's reign, Jones has been fitness coach under a host of big names and played a key role in helping Roberto Di Matteo's unlikely success when he steered a misfiring side to Champions League and FA Cup success in 2012.

PAUL MCGUINNESS

The son of former Manchester United manager Wilf, Paul McGuinness has always had a strong bond with Old Trafford. So it was no surprise that the PE graduate should end up working there as he built a career in the game.

McGuinness junior was on the books at the Red Devils as a youngster in the 80s but failed to make the grade. He went on to play for Crewe Alexandra and Chester City in the Football League.

It was after McGuinness hung up his boots that he really left his mark on United though. He joined the club's academy in 1992 and played a role in the careers of dozens of youngsters coming through the ranks, with 23 going on to become full internationals. It's a proud record that McGuinness added to by leading United to victory in the FA Youth Cup in 2011.

DAN MICCICHE

Credited with being one of the men who helped to hone Tottenham and England star Dele Alli's raw talent, Micciche is renowned as one of the brightest, most forward-thinking British coaches in the modern game.

After working through the ranks at Crystal Palace and Tottenham's academies, Micciche, who studied international management at Loughborough, went to MK Dons to become assistant academy manager. One of a number of Loughborough graduates making a name for himself off the pitch in professional football.

ROB MATTHEWS

Matthews never intended to become a professional footballer. The striker from Slough turned down offers to go into the Football League before he graduated with a geography degree in 1992, then finally signed on the dotted line for Neil Warnock's Notts County. Matthews was a regular goalscorer at Meadow Lane throughout his three years playing for the Magpies and went on to play for seven more Football League clubs, most notably Bury, Stockport County and Hull City. By the time he retired, Matthews had played well over 200 professional matches.

BRADLEY PRITCHARD

Released by Crystal Palace as a teenager, Pritchard was ready to throw in the towel and give up football, but then he landed at Loughborough. Even after enrolling at university, Pritchard needed a little bit of encouragement not to join the hockey team instead.

After a successful Football League career playing for the likes of Charlton Athletic and Leyton Orient, Pritchard must be glad he chose football. An energetic central midfielder, Pritchard benefited from Loughborough's football programme to get into non-league at Nuneaton Borough and Tamworth before making the jump to the professional ranks.

After leaving full-time football in 2016, Pritchard is now training to become a lawyer while turning out for Isthmian League side Greenwich Borough.

TED POWELL

Another one of the feted 1962-63 vintage that included Bob Wilson, Dario Gradi and co, Powell is best known for his impact off the pitch. As an amateur player, Powell did receive international honours though – turning out for the Great Britain Olympic team and earning 51 caps for England Amateurs.

But on the touchline he coached the Malawi national team for six years between 1977 and 1983, and joined an England under-18 side that included Paul Scholes, Sol Campbell and Robbie Fowler, helping them to European Championships. Powell is recognised by many of that side as having had a big impact on their early careers.

DAVE REDDIN

Ever since graduating from Loughborough with a sports science degree in 1991, Reddin's career has been on an upwards trajectory. While his name might not be as well known as some of the footballers who have progressed on the playing side, he has rubbed shoulders with the best: as national fitness coach at the RFU for nearly a decade (including during England's 2003 World Cup win), and as head of performance at the British Olympic Association and FA. He now works as head of team strategy & performance at the FA.

DARREN ROBINSON

As a scholar at Hull City, Darren Robinson thought he was destined to become a professional footballer. But after maintaining his education on the advice of a wise mentor, Robinson found himself at Loughborough looking for a new route into the game he loves.

While Robinson did go on to collect a number of first-team appearances at Chesterfield and Burton Albion, he was preparing for a career in the back room. Armed with a degree and experience as a coach of Loughborough's university team, he forged a path that has seen him work at a host of clubs, including Nottingham Forest, Huddersfield Town, Derby County and Coventry City. Robinson is now head of performance at Birmingham City, where he still preaches the importance of an education for young scholars.

LAWRIE SANCHEZ

Possibly Loughborough's most famous alumni, Sanchez was part of the legendary Crazy Gang squad that led unfashionable Wimbledon to FA Cup glory in 1988. Sanchez's header, which sealed the Dons' cup final victory over favourites Liverpool, has gone down in English football folklore and is replayed annually on screens around the world.

Sanchez is best known for his decade at Wimbledon, but he also spent six years at Reading before moving to south London in 1984. He turned out for Swindon Town and Sligo Rovers before becoming a manager.

Sanchez's penchant for a cup fairytale was realised again in 2001 when he guided third tier Wycombe Wanderers to the FA Cup semi-final, where they lost to his old nemesis Liverpool after a close contest. The Londoner also enjoyed high-profile spells managing at Fulham and the Northern Ireland national team, when he upset the odds once again by masterminding a 1-0 win over Sven-Göran Eriksson's England at Windsor Park.

ROBBIE SIMPSON

Robbie Simpson looked as though he was destined for the top. But after six years as a member of Norwich City's academy, the forward was released and snapped up by Cambridge City. While at the non-leaguers, Simpson continued his education and took a sports science and maths degree at Loughborough University.

Although Simpson remained a Cambridge player (moving to big-city neighbours Cambridge United for his final year), he also joined Loughborough's football programme and won three consecutive BUCS trophies before graduating in 2007. The support network that Loughborough – and higher education – provided was crucial for Simpson's personal development and he went on to become an established Football League star.

At the time of writing, Simpson is currently playing at his seventh professional club, Exeter City, and is best known for his time at Coventry City and Oldham Athletic.

MICHAEL SKUBALA

Loughborough's performance manager at the beginning of the 2016/17 season, Skubala has been involved with the university's football programme for several years. After earning a big reputation in the futsal arena, Skubala was appointed as England's futsal head coach and the FA's elite performance manager for the sport.

TONY STRUDWICK

He might not be a household name, but Tony Strudwick is one of Loughborough's most successful graduates. Now head of performance at Manchester United, Strudwick has worked with the likes of Jose Mourinho and Louis van Gaal during his time at Old Trafford.

It has been quite an ascent for Strudwick since he completed his sports science degree at Loughborough in the late 90s. He went on to be an exercise scientist at Coventry City and the FA, and took on his first senior role as head of fitness and conditioning at West Ham United. Two years at Blackburn Rovers followed, until Manchester United came calling, where he now plays a pivotal role in helping some of the nation's top players get the most out of their games.

ALLEN WADE

A man considered in many quarters to have transformed English football – and not just because he led Loughborough Colleges on their incredible FA Amateur Cup run in 1961. More famously, Wade was FA technical director between 1964 and 1982, and wrote several coaching books that became bibles to some of England's most famous coaches, including Sir Bobby Robson, Don Howe and Roy Hodgson.

As a true mark of Wade's otherworldly insight into the beautiful game at a time when coaching wasn't as widely acknowledged as it is now, some of his books are still in print – decades after they were first published. Most notably, Wade's The FA Guide to Training and Coaching is still a tome that many swear by today.

TONY WAITERS

When a young Tony Waiters first turned out for Loughborough back in the 1950s, he was taking the first steps of an incredible career that would see him make an impact on the international stage – not once, but twice.

After earning a good reputation during an eight-year stay at Blackpool, goalkeeper Waiters was called up to play for England in 1964 and was part of Sir Alf Ramsey's initial 40-man England squad to play in the 1966 World Cup, but missed out in the final selection.

While Waiters was successful on the pitch, he was about to embark on an even more prized role as a coach. After working for the FA and Liverpool, Waiters managed Plymouth Argyle between 1972 and 1977, before heading out to Canada to take charge at Vancouver Whitecaps. He then went on to take the Canadian national team to the 1986 World Cup, the country's best performance, before setting up a successful coaching company in North America.

BOB WILSON

One of the most recognisable faces on Loughborough's alumni wall, Wilson became recognised as a formidable shot-stopper at Arsenal throughout the 1960s and early 70s. Wilson played 234 league matches for the Gunners and continued to coach the club's goalkeepers after hanging up his gloves.

Despite being born in Chesterfield, Wilson received international honours for Scotland – winning two caps for the Tartan Army due to rules allowing players to be eligible for the country of their parents' birth. Wilson continued to be a recognisable face long after his retirement, thanks to television work as a football pundit.

GEORGE WILLIAMS

Williams captained the Scholars in the Midland Football League during his time at university, spending a season with the side. The defender had dropped down several levels after leaving MK Dons in 2012 but found his way back there after bouncing back through higher education.

After impressing at Loughborough, Williams combined studying with playing at Conference North side Worcester City and then stepped up again to move to League One Barnsley. Williams enjoyed a fantastic 2015-16 at Oakwell and helped the Tykes to promotion to the Championship and clinched the Football League Trophy at the showpiece final at Wembley. Williams left Barnsley later that summer and rejoined MK Dons, only four years after leaving them.

INDEX

A

Accam, David — 94, 97
Ackerley, Alex — 76, 115-120, 150, 169, 178-179, 186
AFC Bournemouth — 153
AFC Wulfrunians — 164, 167-168
Afolayan, Dapo — 129-135, 150
AGF Aarhus — 96
Aguero, Sergio — 24
Alexander-Arnold, Trent — 182
Alvechurch — 78, 99, 172
Ancelotti, Carlo — 139, 204
Anderlecht — 13
Antigua & Barbuda — 87-88, 199
Arsenal — 9, 13, 97, 122, 125, 141, 203, 210
Ashton, Danny — 48-49
Aston Villa — 10, 91, 179

B

Baker, Nathan — 133
Bangor City — 192
Barcelona — 140, 153
Barnes, John — 76
Barnes, Tom — 38, 41, 106
Barnet — 203
Barnsley — 58, 211
Barwell — 22
Bedford, Jake — 37, 39
Berwick Rangers — 198
Billericay Town — 71
Birmingham City — 202, 207
Bishop Auckland — 11-12, 32, 181
BK Hacken — 96
Blackburn Rovers — 198, 209
Blackpool — 210
Blunt, Keith — 82-83, 198
Boachie, Joe — 77-79
Boldmere St Michaels — 156, 161
Bowron, Ken — 13, 198
Bradford City — 201
Bradshaw, Alan — 13, 31, 83, 198-199
Braithwaite, Paul — 161
Brenan, Danny — 20, 27, 38-39, 41, 46-47, 70-71, 89, 99, 113-114, 116, 121, 171
Brennan, Karl — 19, 21, 25, 30, 45, 48, 71-79, 104, 108, 163, 165, 169-170, 172
Bridge, Drew — 39, 48, 105-106, 108-109, 149, 156, 172

Brighouse Town 42
Bristol City 97
Brocton 161-164, 167
Brown, Phil 25
BUCS (British Universities and College Sport) 23, 43, 51-52, 62, 64, 68, 70-76, 85-87, 91, 96-97, 111-116, 118-122, 148-150, 155, 190, 192, 201, 208
Bundu, Mustapha 95
Burton Albion 51, 55, 118, 207
Bury 91, 205
Butt, Nicky 83

C

Cale, Andy 84, 199
Camacho, Rafael 186
Campbell, Sol 83, 206
Cambridge City 208
Cambridge United 208
Canada 88, 210
Cardiff City 18
Cardiff Metropolitan University 148-150, 192
Carlisle United 138
Celtic 143-144, 202
Champions League 24, 139-140, 178, 189, 199, 201, 204

Championship 51, 65, 191
Charity Shield 10
Charles-Cook, Regan 130
Charlton Athletic 27, 58, 61, 65, 130, 206
Chelsea 130-131, 134, 140, 153, 179, 204
Chester City 204
Chesterfield 84-86, 199, 207
Chicago Fire 96
Chitiza, Tendai 41
Clapham Rovers 34
Clermont Foot 128
Clough, Brian 158
Coe, Seb 159
Conference North 51, 64, 211
Conference National 60, 65, 82, 129, 188, 197
Conference South 35, 191
Conte, Antonio 140
Cooper, Jake 92
Corinthian Casuals 11, 32
Coventry City 202, 207, 208-209
Coyle, Liam 183
Crane, Tim 81-84
Crewe Alexandra 187, 198-199, 202, 204
Critchley, Neil 187-188

Crookes, Matthew 40, 49,163-164
171, 186

Crystal Palace 61-62, 203,
205-206

Curtis, Tom 63, 84-89, 199

D

Dada, Toluwa 20
Dale, Nathan 72
Danish Superliga 96
Dasaoulu, James 38
Dasaolu, Jeremiah 27, 38-40,
71-72, 78, 89

Davies, Chris 200
Derby County 85, 91,
158, 207

Diacre, Corinne 128
Di Matteo, Roberto 141, 204
Dinsmore, Alex 108, 114, 162-163
Durham University 110-116,
120-121, 148

E

Eagle, Russ 39
Eastern Sports Club 128
East Kilbride 123-124, 126
Edwards, Jake 162
England 9-10, 32, 83, 87, 138,
150-154, 195, 200-202,
206, 208, 210

Ellis, James 62-64, 84-85,
189-196, 200

Enerenadu, Christian 78, 114-115
Erith, Sam 142, 200-201
Europa League 192
Everton 126
Exeter City 34, 58, 97, 181,
194, 208

F

FA, The 13, 15-17, 21, 23, 44,
71, 87, 95, 99, 102,
150-151, 156, 191, 193,
198-199, 202, 204, 209

FA Amateur Cup 11-13, 31-33,
180-181, 209

FA Cup 28-31, 33-42, 50, 86, 93,
99, 141, 199, 204, 207-208

FA Women's Cup 125
Falkirk 124
FA Vase 95, 160
Fee, Greg 201
Fletcher, Tom 157-165, 179
Football League 24, 30, 56-58, 61,
64-67, 84, 90, 94-95, 98, 179, 184,
186, 188, 193, 196, 203-206, 208

Fowler, Robbie 206
France 189
Froggatt, Richard 106
Frost, James 108
Fulham 136, 191, 200, 208
Futsal 22-23, 29, 150-155, 209

G

Gerrard, Steven 177-181, 187-188
Ghana 94, 97-98
Gillingham 56, 61
Goodwyn, Alfred 33-34
Goold, Nick 72-73, 78
Gradi, Dario 31, 82-83, 202, 206
Grant, Sirdic Adjei 94-100
Grantham Town 89
Grays Athletic 71
Great Britain Universities 22, 84, 189-190, 200, 203
Greaves, Richard 100
Green, Geoffrey 11-13
Greenwich Borough 67, 206
Gresley FC 41
Grimsby Town 123

H

Halil, Bekir 49
Harborough Town 27

Hartpury College 94-98
Harris, Ben 41
Harris, Dan 143-147, 202
Harrogate Town 43
Hawkins, Richard 202-203
Hayes & Yeading 65
Heanor Town 80-84, 89, 104
Hednesford Town 89, 113-114, 171
Helsingborg 96
Hereford 95-96, 99
Hibernian 125
Hiddink, Guus 141
Hill, Josh 36, 39
Hinckley United 22
Hines, Barry 82-83, 203
Hitchin Town 11, 32, 180
Hodgson, Roy 201, 209
Holland, Steve 141
Honduras 88
Howarth, Lee 203
Howe, Eddie 153
Huddersfield Town 57, 207
Hughes, Charles 204
Hughes, Will 154
Hull City 25, 42-43, 91, 138, 201, 205, 207
Hull University 195
Hulse, Mark 203

Hyde United 187

I
Iceland 155
Inglethorpe, Alex 181-182
Irvine, Alan 18
Ivanusch, Christoph 52-56, 184-185

J
Jackson, Joe 19, 48, 72, 107, 156
Johnson, Alex 163, 171
Jones, Chris 140-142, 204

K
Kane, Herbie 186
Kearins, Dave 38
Kelleher, Caoimhin 183-184
Kennington Oval 33-34
Kerr, Shelley 122-128, 191-192, 194
Kim, Jae Heon 19-20
Kilmarnock 125
Kouadio, Joe 26-27

L
L'Ghoul, Nassim 19
Langwith Road 40-41

Last, Ben 115-116, 149, 163-164, 172
Lauchlan, Martin 123
Leeds Metropolitan University 96, 195
Legg, Elliott 48-49, 70-71, 77, 172, 184
Leicester City 59, 75-76, 91, 137-140, 147, 179, 201
Leicestershire Senior League 31
Leigh Genesis 187
Leyton Orient 61, 66, 206
Lilley, Kyle 39
Liverpool 53, 76, 177-188, 200, 203, 207, 210
Lolley, Joe 57
Long Eaton United 161
Longstaff, Lewis 184
Lorient 97
Loughborough Colleges 9-13, 16, 31-33, 209
Loughborough Dynamo 104, 160, 200
Loughborough Students' Union 179
Loughborough University Stadium 29, 35-40, 51, 80-85, 89-93, 157, 177

Lowland Football League
123-124,192

Lucozade Sport 145-146

Luton Town 37, 56-57, 61, 91, 116, 184

Lye Town 167-168, 185

Lyon 18

Lyng, Joe 156

M

Mackarness, Charles 34

Mahrez, Riyad 139

Major League Soccer (MLS)
96, 132-133

Malawi 206

Malmo 82, 198

Manchester City 98, 142, 201

Manchester United 9-10, 84, 90, 117, 142, 179, 181, 202-205, 209

Mansfield Town 35, 201, 203

Maradona, Diego 129-130

Marseille 18

Martinez, Roberto 153

Matthews, Rob 84, 90-92, 205

McGuinness, Paul 84, 204-205

McLaren, Stuart 161

McMahon, Paul 164

Meese, Dave 48-49

Melbourne City 201

Micciche, Dan 205

Middlesbrough 86

Midland Combination 85

Midland Football League 16, 23-24, 36, 43, 50-51, 63, 68-69, 72-76, 80, 88, 95, 100, 112-113, 133, 148, 156, 167, 184, 211

Miller, Liam 183-184

Milligan, Jack 76

Minehane, Sam 59

Miveld, Lee 105

MK Dons 58, 205, 211

Moli, David 55

Moor Green 31-32

Morpeth Town 96

Mourinho, Jose 39, 141, 203, 209

Mullins, Mitch 37, 39

N

Napean, Charles 34

Neil, Alex 18

Neville, Gary 83

Neville, Phil 83

Newcastle United 198, 203

New York City FC 201

Newton, Eddie 141

Nike Academy 15,18-20, 25, 111-113

Nisbett, Marvin 48

Nortey, Nortei 133

Northern Ireland 89, 208

North Ferriby Town 43

Norwich City 18, 208

Nottingham Forest 22, 158, 207

Nottingham Trent 196

Notts County 90-91, 179, 205

Nti, Daniel 59

Nuneaton Town 54-56, 64, 206

Nurse, Ricky 73, 77, 79, 104, 170

O

O'Keefe, Conor 20, 37, 48, 72-73, 92, 104, 156, 162, 172, 183-184, 186

Oldham Athletic 56, 69, 120, 208

Ontario High School 132

Osborne, Liam 35, 39

Ostersunds FK 96, 191, 195

Oxford University 33-35, 196

P

Panama 88

Patton, Frederick 34

Pearman, John 179-181

Pearson, Laurie 171

Pearson, Nigel 138-139, 201

Peterborough United 27, 202-203

Plymouth Argyle 210

Pochettino, Mauricio 153

Portsmouth 84

Potter, Graham 96, 195

Powell, Hope 123

Powell, Ted 83, 206

Poxon, Jack 29, 68-69, 78-79, 116, 120, 184

Premier League 18, 24, 36, 91, 94, 97, 103, 130, 134, 136, 139 140-142, 148, 154, 178, 186, 190, 201, 204

Preston North End 201

Pritchard, Bradley 58, 61-67, 81, 194, 206

Q

Quorn 69-73, 75, 77-79

R

Ranieri, Claudio 140

Rankin, Tom 70, 105-107

Rashford, Marcus 179

Read, Alex 92, 100, 106, 108, 120, 162

Read, Liam 172

Reading 182, 206, 208

Reddin, Dave 206-207
Redditch United 27
Reeves, Matt 136-140, 142, 201
Reid, Peter 102
Rennie, Dave 137
Right to Dream Academy 94-98
Robinson, Darren 207
Rocester 101-109
Rochdale 133-134, 152
Rodgers, Brendan 200
Rogic, Tom 18
Ronaldinho 153
Roome, Oliver 107
Royal Engineers 33-34
Rugby Town 22
Russia 189-190

S

Sanchez, Lawrie 180, 207
Sanusi, Hafeez 70, 72, 92
Scholes, Paul 206
Scotland 13, 122, 203, 211
Seoul E-Land 143-144, 146, 201
Shepshed Dynamo 161, 166-176, 178
Skubala, Michael 21-26, 28-30, 37, 42-45, 49, 58-60, 70-71, 76, 101-102, 104, 108,

114-116, 118, 150-155, 209
Shawbury United 167-168, 172
Shaw Lane Aquaforce 42-44
Shearer, Alan 145
Shearer, Luke 47
Sheffield Wednesday 201
Sheffield United 202
Shirebrook Town 30-31, 35-41, 50, 56
Simpson, Robbie 58, 81, 194, 208
Sligo Rovers 208
Smith, Leighton 78
Smythe, Martyn 108
Solihull Moors 129-130, 133-135, 150
Southampton 138
Southern Premier League 196
Southgate, Gareth 151-152, 200
Spartak Moscow 96
Sporting Khalsa 45-49
Stallan, James 48-49, 104, 108, 115-116, 121, 150
Stalybridge Celtic 82
St George's Park 15-19, 25-27, 29, 154
Stiles, Nobby 9
Stirling University 68-70, 72, 77, 122-128, 192, 194

Stock, Mat 17-19, 27, 46, 50-51, 82, 104-105, 111, 168, 188

Stockport County 59, 205

Stone, Aidan 163-164

Strudwick, Tony 142, 209

Sunderland 57

Sutton United 129

Swansea City 200

Swindon Town 97, 208

Switch the Play 191, 193, 200

T

Tamworth 65, 206

Taylor, Jake 163, 168

Team Bath 34-35, 191, 194

The New Saints (TNS) 199

Tisdale, Paul 34, 194-195

Tividale 167

Toronto FC 132

Tottenham Hotspur 179, 198, 205

Trotman, Liam 37, 40, 56-58, 92, 116, 164, 184

Tuck, Dan 104-105

U

USA 88

V

Vancouver Whitecaps 210

Vardy, Jamie 139

Viking 198

Villas-Boas, Andre 141

VS Rugby 160

W

Wade, Allen 13, 209-210

Waiters, Tony 84, 88, 210

Wales 34, 89

Walsall Wood 167

Wanderers 34

Ward-Cochrane, Ben 20, 106, 108, 172, 183, 186

Waris, Abdul Majeed 18, 94, 97

Warnock, Neil 90-91, 205

Watford 154

Watmore, Duncan 57

Watson, Gordon 160-165, 179

Welcombe, Nicholas 162

Welsh Premier Division 149, 193, 199

Wembley 95-96, 160, 181

West Bromwich Albion 143, 179, 202

Westfields 93-100, 167

West Ham United 209

Wilson, Bob   9-13, 31-32, 82-83,
              180, 203, 206, 210-211
Wilkinson, Danny   42-49
Williams, George   58, 81, 211
Wimbledon   207-208
Woking   135
Wolstenholme, Kenneth   32
Women's Super League   124
Woodburn, Ben   182
Worcester City   131
World Cup   32, 87-88, 97,
                      151-152, 210
World University Games   189-190
Wright, Danny   29, 77
Wycombe Wanderers   208

Y

Yeun-ting, Chan   128
York City   59

Printed in Great Britain
by Amazon